The Manosphere

Also from EATMS Productions

Books on power, survival, women's autonomy, and the systems shaping modern America.

Nonfiction

Billionaires, Capitalism, and Power

Evil and the Mountain Ungreed
Self Help for American Billionaires
Selfish Steve and the Ivory Tower
Tariffs, Taxes, & Face-Eating Leopards
Ban Billionaires: Fascism Fix

Fascism, Religion, and Cultural Control

Self Help for the Manosphere
Fascism 2025
Fascism & the Perverts & the Greed Virus
Christian Fascism Marriage Book
Tyranny, Table Manners, & Tiramisu

Guides for Women's Autonomy and Protection

How to Survive in Post-America as a Woman
Project 2025 American Drag
4B – Burn, Ban, Boycott, Build
4B OG – So No Go GYN
I'm Glad He's Dead

Analysis of Authoritarian Project 2025

Project 2025: The Blueprint
Project 2025: The List
Project 2025, Christian Dumb Dumbs, & The Republican Agenda
Fascism, Project 2025, & The Pinkprint

Modern Rewrites for Women

Stoic Principles Reimagined
Siddhartha Reimagined
The Prince Reimagined for Women
The Art of War Reimagined for Women
The Jungle Reimagined
The Constitution Reimagined for Women

Machine Learning Series

AI, Bitcoin, Nostr for Women
AI, Safety, & Security for Women
AI, Anxiety, & Health for Women
AI, Kids, & Family Safety for Women
AI, Creativity, & Personal Expression for Women
AI, Independent Work, & Parallel Power for Women

Social Systems Series

Emotional Labor for Women
Household Power for Women
Workplace Power for Women
Medical Bias for Women
Aging Systems for Women
Recovery Systems for Women

Fiction

Dystopian Stories of Resistance and Collapse

Propaganda Paige & the Missing Prosperity
Propaganda Paige & the TIDE Manifesto
Propaganda Paige & the Shadow Cartographers
Propaganda Paige & the Prosperity Alliance
Propaganda Paige & the Shattered Truth
Propaganda Paige & the Rising TIDE
Propaganda Paige & the Last Bastion
Propaganda Paige & the Dawn of Prosperity
Project 2025: Dorian — The Last Men
Project 2025: Boy — A Last Men Novel

Self Help For The Manosphere

Self Help is Performative Acquiescence To a "Broken" System
(SHIPA TABS) 2

A Laughing Matter
A Parody

by
Esme Mees
& Biddie Beuys

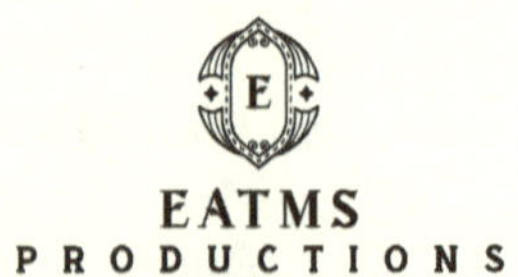

EATMS
PRODUCTIONS

Copyright © 2024 Eatms Productions
All rights reserved.

This title is part of an ongoing body of work. All EATMS Productions titles, across all series, authors, and formats, are components of a single connected project.

No part of this book may be reproduced, or stored in a retrieval system, or transmitted in any form or by any means, electronic, mechanical, photocopying, recording, or otherwise, without express permission in writing from the publisher.

This book is a work of opinion and creative interpretation. While some names and events may be referenced or alluded to, any claims made are based on publicly available information and are intended as satire, parody, or commentary on societal and political issues. The content should not be interpreted as factual assertions about any individual or entity. The author does not intend to defraud, defame, or mislead, and encourages readers to form their own conclusions. Any resemblance to real persons, living or dead, is purely coincidental unless explicitly noted otherwise.

ISBN 978-1-966014-08-9

Cover, interior design, interior prints by: Esme Mees

eatms@pm.me
www.eatms.me

Printed in the United States of America.

When culture is based on a dominator model, not only will it be violent, but it will frame all relationships as power struggles.

— bell hooks

The manosphere is a sprawling and often contentious digital ecosystem where men congregate to discuss issues related to masculinity, relationships, and societal roles. On the surface, it presents itself as a space for men to express concerns about challenges they face, from perceived biases in family courts to struggles with identity in a rapidly changing world. However, much of the discourse within the manosphere veers into adversarial territory, framing gender dynamics as a zero-sum game and fostering antagonistic views toward women and feminism.

Within this space, various subcultures flourish, each with its own ideology and rhetoric. One prominent group consists of self-proclaimed "pick-up artists" (PUAs), who offer advice on seduction and dating, often reducing relationships to transactional conquests. Another faction, the "men's rights activists" (MRAs), claims to advocate for legitimate issues such as mental health, male suicide rates, and biases in custody battles but frequently devolves into anti-feminist diatribes. Then there are the so-called "red-pilled" communities, which posit that society is rigged against men and encourage a worldview steeped in conspiracy, grievance, and a rigid return to traditional gender roles.

The manosphere has become a fertile ground for the amplification of toxic masculinity, providing validation for frustrations and fears while often reinforcing harmful stereotypes. Its narratives can blur the line between legitimate grievances and the outright demonization of women, painting them as either oppressors or objects to be controlled. The echo-chamber effect magnifies these views, creating insular communities where dissent is rare and extremist ideologies can thrive unchecked. Despite its diversity, the manosphere is united by a common thread: a reactionary response to the perceived loss of male dominance in society. What might have begun as a space for introspection has, in many cases, devolved into a hotbed of resentment, misrepresentation, and regressive thinking.

Table of Contents

Introduction
Welcome to the Bropacalypse

The "Victory" That Burns

Congratulations, bros, you've done it. The dystopia you always dreamed of is finally here. After years of whining in echo chambers and trading memes about traditional values, you've reclaimed your place at the top of the societal pyramid, or so you think. The 2024 election was your crowning achievement, a seismic political victory that unleashed Project 2025 and reshaped the nation in your image. And what an image it is: a scorched, barren wasteland where women are stripped of their autonomy, social safety nets have been shredded like yesterday's Twitter controversies, and corporations now rule with the benevolence of rabid wolves. You should be celebrating. This is your moment, right? But as you puff out your chest and bask in the glow of your newfound power, let's pause for a moment of clarity: you're already losing.

This "victory" isn't the triumphant return to glory you'd imagined, it's a Pyrrhic one, where the cost of winning is higher than you ever anticipated. The world you've created is crumbling faster than your last NFT investment. Women are out of the workforce, forced into a grotesque caricature of 1950s domesticity, but guess what? The economy isn't doing any better without them. Social safety nets? Gone, of course, because real men don't need handouts, right? Except now, there's no one to catch you when the free market eats you alive. You wanted unfettered capitalism, and now the corporations are feasting on the scraps of democracy like vultures at a carcass. Meanwhile, you're left holding the bill and wondering why the grindset isn't working out as planned. But hey, at least you still have your crypto wallet, or what's left of it after the latest crash. You might not be able to afford gas or groceries, but you can still buy a JPEG of a pixelated ape for what was once the price of a car.

Let's talk about the landscape you've built. It's a vision of America you once sold to yourselves as a paradise for strong men and submissive women, but it's looking a lot more like a poorly managed dumpster fire. Women's rights? Decimated. Autonomy? A relic of the past. You've reduced half the population to second-class citizens, and yet you're still complaining about how oppressed you feel. Social progress is now a dirty word, banned from polite conversation, replaced by an endless loop of platitudes about masculinity, strength, and the good old days that never actually existed. Corporations, no longer constrained by pesky regulations or taxes, are running wild, selling off what's left of public infrastructure and turning every aspect of your life into a subscription service. Want clean water? That'll be $29.99 a month. Thinking about getting a job? Better hope your social score doesn't tank when you post another rant about how the matriarchy is ruining your life.

And here's the kicker: the men who once howled at the supposed injustices of feminism and progress are now the loudest voices of victimhood. Enter "Men Too," the crowning jewel of your movement, a farce of epic proportions. Picture this: a group of self-declared alphas standing on gilded soapboxes, shouting into megaphones about how hard it is to be a man in the very system they built. You've turned victimhood into a brand, complete with hashtags, merch, and rallies where the attendees outnumber the brain cells in the room. Men Too is your cry for help, a laughable attempt to position yourselves as oppressed in a society you control. And the world? It's laughing. Loudly.

Let's not overlook the absurdity of your newfound power. You've torn down the pillars of equality, clawed your way to the top of the social heap, and yet here you are, still unsatisfied. The dream you sold yourselves, a world where men rule unchallenged and women quietly comply, has turned out to be less of a utopia and more of a waking nightmare. You thought power would make you happy, but it seems to have only amplified your insecurities. You're kings of a collapsing castle, clutching at the remnants of your misguided ideals while the walls crumble around you. And now, instead of introspection, you double down on your grievances, shouting louder and louder in the hopes that someone, anyone, will take you seriously. Spoiler alert: we're not taking you seriously. We're laughing. Because, honestly, what else is there to do?

This is where our story begins, in the ashes of your supposed triumph. This book is your mirror, bros, and it doesn't blink. It's a survival guide for the world you created, a world that is eating you alive one policy at a time. But make no mistake, this isn't a guide to help you win. It's a guide to help you laugh, at yourselves, at the absurdity of it all, and at the fact that the systems you championed are the very ones now crushing you under their weight. You wanted unfettered capitalism, and now you're drowning in it. You wanted traditional gender roles, but the women you longed to control have left you behind. You wanted freedom, but only for yourselves, and now even that is slipping through your fingers.

From the rise of Men Too to the downfall of your crypto empires, from your gym obsessions to your doomed attempts at Brotopia, this book will explore the comedy and tragedy of your world in equal measure. We'll dissect your alpha posturing, your fragile egos, and your relentless quest to blame everyone but yourselves for the mess you're in. We'll show you how the very ideals you cling to are the ones pulling you under, and we'll do it all with a smile and a well-timed punchline. Because let's be honest: the joke is on you.

So yes, congratulations on your victory. Bask in it. Revel in the ashes of the society you claimed to save. But don't get too comfortable, because the ride is far from over. The road ahead is steep, the descent is fast, and the brakes? Well, those were sold off for spare parts a long time ago. Welcome to the Bropacalypse, gentlemen. You built it, you broke it, and now you get to live in it. And for the rest of us? We'll be over here with our popcorn, watching the show and laughing at the irony of it all. Because while the flames are high, the comedy is higher, and the world you've created is nothing if not a farce of epic proportions. Good luck, bros. You're going to need it.

Anatomy of the Bropacalypse

Let's take a moment to unpack how you've arrived at this flaming wreckage of a society, shall we? It didn't happen overnight, though you'd love to believe it did, some grand feminist conspiracy swooping in like a cartoon villain to undermine your fragile sense of purpose. No, this particular disaster has been brewing for years, maybe even decades, with roots firmly planted in a culture that values power over compassion, dominance over cooperation, and the outdated belief that masculinity is measured by how loudly you can yell over someone else. You didn't just stumble into the Bropacalypse; you built it. Brick by brick, tweet by tweet, podcast by podcast, you laid the foundation. And not only did you construct it, you made sure to live-stream its grand opening, complete with hashtags and sponsorship deals.

You've spent years peddling the idea that society is rigged against you, that feminism is a zero-sum game where every step forward for women is a step back for men. You wore toxic masculinity like a badge of honor, turning it into a rallying cry because facing your insecurities was too daunting. You found comfort in the digital echo chambers of the manosphere, where garden-variety frustration festered into full-blown rage. You ranted about the courts being unfair, about women taking all the good jobs, about a world that no longer catered to your fragile ego. And you didn't notice, or didn't care, that your demands were rooted in nostalgia for a time that never existed, a Leave It to Beaver fantasy where men ruled unchallenged, women stayed quiet, and everything was just peachy for the guys at the top.

And let's not forget your political choices. You voted out of anger rather than thought, rallied behind leaders who spat out the right buzzwords instead of offering real solutions. You cheered as they gutted healthcare, underfunded schools, and deregulated everything in sight. Who needs functional public systems when you have the free market, right? You bought into the fantasy that unfettered capitalism would reward your hustle and that patriarchal dominance would restore your sense of control. But instead, you got a system designed to chew you up and spit you out. Now you sit in the wreckage, shouting into the void about the very policies you championed, blaming anyone but yourself for the fallout.

And then there are the key players in this farce, you and your fellow architects of the Bropacalypse. Let's start with the alpha wannabes. You strut and preen like peacocks, living for three-hour podcasts about why women should smile more. Your dominance begins and ends with your ability to complain into a microphone. Then there are the crypto bros, who saw Bitcoin as their golden ticket to freedom, until the market crashed, leaving you clutching digital Monopoly money. The pick-up artists? Still out there selling courses on how to "neg" women into submission while wondering why you're perpetually alone. And of course, the men's rights activists, tirelessly whining about alimony and why society doesn't respect your fedoras. You are the stars of this tragicomedy, shouting the loudest and thinking the least, now drowning in the ruins you've made.

Here's the cruel irony: the systems you championed, unfettered capitalism, hyper-individualism, and patriarchal dominance, are the very ones crushing you. You cried for fewer regulations, and now your crypto dreams have evaporated, unprotected from the market forces you worshipped. You demanded hyper-individualism, and now you're isolated, left to stew in your own loneliness. You preached patriarchal dominance, only to find that the women you wanted to control simply opted out of playing along. You've become victims of your own hubris, shouting that women are "taking everything" while ignoring the simpler truth: you've taken yourself out of the game.

The contradictions at the heart of your worldview are almost too easy to mock. You preach self-reliance but are the first to beg for sympathy when things don't go your way. You demand traditional gender roles while failing to live up to even the most basic expectations of those roles. You rail against feminism as if it's a personal affront, yet secretly long for the emotional labor of women to soothe your insecurities. You champion free speech but crumble under the slightest criticism. Every action you take is a satirical mirror of the strength and dominance you think you embody, reflecting instead the fragile ego you so desperately try to protect.

This is the anatomy of your Bropacalypse: a culture that fed on grievance and insecurity, a political system that pandered to your worst instincts, and a cast of characters who can't see the forest for the trees, or the flames. You wanted control, but now you're trapped by it. You wanted power, but now it's eating you alive. And the rest of us? We're just watching, popcorn in hand, waiting for the next act in this circus of self-destruction. Because let's face it: if it weren't so devastating, it would be hilarious. And maybe it's both. You wanted to bend the world to your will, but all you've done is create a farce of epic proportions. Bravo. Take a bow. You've earned it.

Welcome to Your Survival Guide

Welcome, bros, to the part where we explain why this book exists, not that you asked. Let's be clear from the outset: this isn't your traditional self-help guide. We're not here to fix you. Honestly, there's no fixing what's already been burned to the ground. What we're offering instead is a satirical roadmap to navigate the smoldering ruins you've built for yourselves. Think of it less as a guide to thriving and more as a guide to laughing while you struggle. Because if there's one thing left in this post-2025 world, it's the endless comedy of watching you trip over your own hubris. So, no, this book won't save you, but it will let you chuckle at the absurdity of it all, and trust us, you're going to need a sense of humor to survive the mess you've made.

Why do you need this book? Because the systems you worshipped have turned on you. Your idols, unfettered capitalism, hyper-individualism, and patriarchal dominance, have shown their true faces, and surprise! They're not kind. They're not fair. They're not even functional. You created a world where empathy is weakness, cooperation is betrayal, and strength is measured by how loudly you can yell about how unfair everything is. And yet, here you are, whining into the void about how hard it is to be a man. You demand sympathy while mocking those who need it, preach traditional values while failing to embody any of them, and cry oppression from atop the very systems you claim to control. That's why this book exists, not to help you climb out of the hole you've dug, but to sit at the edge with popcorn and point out the irony of you complaining about the dirt.

What's inside this guide to the Bropacalypse, you ask? Oh, only the greatest hits of your movement. We'll start with your alpha posturing, the endless chest-thumping and pseudo-philosophy that props up your fragile egos. You're kings of a crumbling castle, convinced that dominance is your birthright even as the walls fall down around you. Then we'll move on to your gym obsessions, where muscles become the substitute for emotional intelligence. You can deadlift a small car, but can you process the fact that your relationships are falling apart? Didn't think so.

Next, we'll take a tour of your doomed Brotopias, those dreamlands of male-only utopia where everything should work perfectly, if only someone had thought to bring a wrench or learn how to cook. Spoiler alert: Brotopia is less a paradise and more a cautionary tale about what happens when you trade cooperation for competition. From there, we'll dive into the comedy goldmine that is "Men Too," the movement where oppressors demand pity, insisting they're the real victims. Nothing screams empowerment like gathering in a room full of bros to whine about how hard it is to be a man in a world where women have no rights. Truly inspiring.

And, of course, we'll tackle your endless victim complex, the way you've managed to twist every failure of your own making into someone else's fault. Your crypto empire collapsed? Blame feminism. Your dating life is in shambles? Clearly, it's because women are too empowered, not because you thought "negging" was a viable strategy. Your career stalled? Must be cancel culture, not the fact that you spend more time ranting online than doing actual work. It's a masterclass in delusion, and we're here to document every moment of it.

The central punchline of this book, and make no mistake, the joke is on you, is that the manosphere has destroyed the very things it claimed to protect. You wanted strong families, but your disdain for women and obsession with dominance has left you isolated. You wanted economic freedom, but your blind faith in deregulation has gutted the systems that kept you afloat. You wanted respect, but you've done everything in your power to ensure you'll never be taken seriously. In your quest to reclaim a mythical golden age of masculinity, you've managed to undermine not just women, but yourselves. And now, all that's left is the rubble, and the comedy.

So, here's our invitation to keep reading. Will this book save you? No. It's far too late for that. But it will give you something to laugh about while the ship sinks. And honestly, laughter is the only lifeboat left in the Bropacalypse. So pull up a chair, crack open whatever protein shake or overpriced whiskey you think makes you look manly, and settle in. You've earned this moment of reflection, whether you like it or not. The flames are high, the irony is higher, and, bros, trust us, you'll need this book more than you think. Enjoy the ride.

Feel Free to Draw a Picture of Your Self Delusions Below

Chapter 1
Alpha Male Apocalypse
How to Dominate a Burnt Out Society

The Alpha Illusion

The Alpha Illusion is your ultimate mythology, isn't it? A desperate attempt to craft an identity that offers structure and validation in a world that no longer worships at the altar of your presumed dominance. You cling to the term "alpha," borrowed from a long-debunked theory about wolf pack hierarchies. Fun fact: the very scientist who coined the term later admitted wolves don't actually organize their lives around a single dominant figure bullying the rest into submission. But science isn't your strong suit, is it? Instead, you gleefully snatched up this pseudo-scientific concept, polished it into something toxic, and wielded it as both a badge of honor and a marketing tool. To you, the alpha male is the paragon of masculinity: strong, assertive, unemotional, and above all, dominant. In reality, it's nothing but a fantasy, an empty suit of armor you clamber into, clanking loudly to drown out the echoes of your own inadequacies.

Let's talk about how absurd this archetype becomes in the context of the crumbling society you now find yourself in. The infrastructure that once upheld your delusions of grandeur is gone, burned to the ground by the very policies you championed. What does it mean to be an alpha when the gyms are closed because the deregulated power grid failed? When your crypto empire collapses into digital dust, taking your self-worth along with it? When the women you assumed would line up to bask in your aura of dominance are too busy organizing underground networks to reclaim their rights? You're not leading a pack, my friend. You're wandering through a wasteland, shouting at the ruins, still convinced society just doesn't appreciate you enough.

And your methods for asserting alpha dominance? Ridiculous and ineffective, yet deeply revealing. Let's start with your podcast, the sacred altar of the manosphere. You set up a cheap microphone in your basement and rant for hours about feminists, "cancel culture," and modern dating, peppering your monologue with references to obscure philosophers you've never actually read. Your audience? A handful of equally lost souls nodding along because your words validate their frustrations. Then there's the gym culture, where you pump iron in the endless pursuit of gains. You might be able to bench press a small car, but you've yet to figure out how to have a conversation that isn't about you. And let's not forget your beloved crypto hustle, nothing screams dominance like investing your life savings in speculative digital currencies, only to watch them tank while you scramble to explain how this is all part of the master plan.

Ah, but the crown jewel of your alpha performance is your self-proclaimed status as a "provider." You parade this title like it's proof of your superiority, as though declaring it makes it true. Let's be honest: what are you really providing? Excuses for your failures? Unsolicited opinions about how women should live their lives? A steady stream of cringe-worthy Instagram posts about the grindset? Meanwhile, your mom's still making your dinner, and your credit score is hovering between "please stop" and "no." The contradiction is almost poetic. The louder you proclaim your dominance, the more obvious it becomes that you have no idea how to achieve it.

This is the heart of the alpha male illusion: it's not just a flawed ideal, it's a tragicomic exercise in self-delusion. You aspire to rule a world you can barely navigate, clinging to outdated notions of power and control while your personal life crumbles under the weight of your own contradictions. You project strength while radiating insecurity, demand respect while offering none, and preach self-reliance while leaning heavily on systems and people you claim to despise. It's not strength, it's a spectacle, a pageant of fragile egos parading in ill-fitting suits of imagined authority.

The satire here is almost too easy, but it's necessary. Examining your obsession with the alpha male archetype means holding up a mirror to your most glaring hypocrisies. You talk about dominance, but what you really crave is validation. You claim to be a leader, but you're just a follower in a pyramid scheme of toxic masculinity, climbing toward an imaginary peak. The grindset never stops, but neither does the insecurity. As you chase the mirage of alpha status, you leave a trail of failed podcasts, abandoned gym memberships, and overdrafted bank accounts in your wake.

The systems you believed would elevate you are the same ones now crushing you. You cheered for deregulation, and now your crypto empire lies in ruins. You demanded hyper-individualism, but here you are, isolated and angry. You preached dominance, only to find that those you hoped to dominate have opted out entirely. You've become a victim of your own hubris, trapped in a self-perpetuating loop of disappointment and blame.

The tactics you've embraced, the self-inflicted wounds you refuse to acknowledge, and the absurdity of a worldview so blind to its own contradictions are all part of the farce. The alpha male apocalypse isn't a triumph or a tragedy, it's a joke, and the punchline is you. Welcome to your grindset, bro. Let's see how long you can keep pretending it works.

The Grindset Fallacy

Your devotion to the grindset is nothing short of religious, a creed etched into the sweaty leather of your weightlifting gloves and whispered fervently into the microphones of your low-budget podcasts. The hustle never stops, does it? Because stopping is for losers. Every waking moment must be dedicated to the pursuit of financial dominance, physical perfection, and, of course, the elusive title of "alpha." Sleep? That's for the weak. Relationships? A distraction. Fulfillment? Who has time for that when there's another poorly researched YouTube video on passive income streams waiting for you? Grindset culture is your gospel, promising salvation through endless effort, but instead of delivering rewards, it leads you to burnout, alienation, and an overwhelming sense of inadequacy.

Let's talk about the hustle culture trap you've walked right into. You wear exhaustion like a badge of honor, treating self-destruction as a necessary stepping stone to success. In your world, every minute not spent "leveling up" is a wasted opportunity, and every failure is proof that you're not hustling hard enough. Never mind that the grind rarely gives you the riches you were promised; the mere act of grinding has become the performance, a pantomime of progress that keeps you locked in a cycle of endless striving. You're on a treadmill to nowhere, but you tell yourself it's all part of the process, even as your knees give out and your dreams collapse under the weight of your delusions. You mistake busyness for productivity, effort for achievement, and suffering for strength. Here's the truth you're ignoring: the grind isn't making you stronger, it's grinding you down.

Nowhere is this clearer than in your obsession with crypto, the sacred altar of grindset culture. You've elevated digital currencies to a near-mythical status, promising yourself that Bitcoin, or, let's be honest, one of the countless centralized scams you got duped into, will be your golden ticket to alpha supremacy. Sure, Bitcoin might have some decentralized integrity, but most of what you're chasing? It's a dumpster fire of Ponzi schemes and rug pulls masquerading as innovation. You pour your life savings into tokens named after dog breeds, convinced you've outsmarted the system, only to watch your so-called fortune vanish overnight. But do you admit defeat? Of course not. You insist it's all part of the master plan, a temporary dip in a long-term strategy that will eventually prove your brilliance. Meanwhile, your portfolio is in ruins, your trust in humanity is shattered, and you cling to the illusion because the alternative, admitting you've been played, is too devastating to bear.

The tragedy of your grindset isn't just in its futility; it's in its performative nature. This isn't about genuine ambition or self-improvement for you. It's about projecting an image of strength and success at all costs. Performative masculinity rules your life, dictating that every action must reinforce the illusion of dominance. Social media is your stage, a carefully curated gallery of gym selfies, motivational quotes, and vague boasts about business ventures that don't actually exist. Behind the scenes, though, the cracks are glaringly obvious. Your relationships are strained or nonexistent because emotional intimacy would mean slowing down, and you're too busy perfecting your brand. Your health deteriorates because grinding means skipping sleep, downing pre-workout shakes, and ignoring basic self-care. Your finances are a mess because you're more interested in chasing the next big thing than building a stable foundation. But none of this matters to you as long as the façade holds. You're so desperate to convince yourself and your equally deluded peers that you're winning, you've completely lost sight of what winning even means.

And when the grind inevitably fails to deliver, as it always does, you shift the blame elsewhere. It's not your fault, is it? Of course not. The world is rigged against you. Feminists, society, cancel culture, they're the ones to blame. When your business collapses, it's because the system is broken. When you can't form meaningful relationships, it's because women are too empowered. When you're unhappy, it's because the world just doesn't appreciate real men anymore. You refuse to acknowledge that your own choices, investing in scams, prioritizing image over substance, treating people as tools, are the root of your problems. Instead, you double down on your grievances, turning failure into a badge of honor and victimhood into a rallying cry.

The grindset fallacy perfectly encapsulates your contradictions. You promise yourself empowerment but deliver exhaustion. You demand self-reliance but desperately seek the approval of others. You preach strength but thrive on insecurity. At the heart of it all is a devastating truth you refuse to face: the grind isn't solving your problems, it's creating them. You've built your identity around this treadmill to nowhere, and you're too busy running to notice you're not getting anywhere. So, the grind goes on, a relentless march toward burnout, failure, and, if you're lucky, the faintest glimmer of self-awareness. But let's not hold our breath. After all, there's always another crypto token to chase, another hustle to fake, and another excuse to make. Welcome to your grindset. May your pre-workout supplements and shaky self-confidence carry you as far as this delusion allows.

How to Fake It Until You Break It

You, the modern alpha male, self-styled king of your domain, have an interesting way of proving your dominance: through the fine art of interruption. Conversations aren't collaborative exchanges for you, they're battlegrounds. Every sentence spoken by someone else is just another threat you need to neutralize. Women, naturally, are your primary targets. Why let them finish a thought when you can swoop in, midsentence, with an unsolicited opinion or a correction that isn't even accurate? You call it "manning up." The rest of us? We know it as "mansplaining." And you don't stop there. This behavior isn't confined to casual settings; the workplace is fair game too. Your interruptions don't just silence women, they broadcast, loudly and obnoxiously, that you're not here to listen, learn, or collaborate. You're here to dominate, even if what you're saying is as empty as your self-awareness.

But don't kid yourself that this is just about women. Your interruptions extend to anyone unlucky enough to share a meeting room, dinner table, or group chat with you. Your conversational toolkit is limited but effective in one way: it ensures that you're the loudest voice in the room, even when you have nothing meaningful to contribute. Listening? That's for betas. But here's the irony, clear to anyone paying attention: the louder you shout, the more obvious it becomes that you're terrified of being ignored. Your so-called dominance through interruption isn't power, it's insecurity, broadcast in Dolby Surround Sound. The more you assert yourself, the less seriously anyone takes you.

And then there's your obsession with being a "provider." You tell yourself this title is about stability and leadership, but let's be honest, it's more about projecting an image of success than actually achieving it. You're not providing security for anyone, not even yourself. What you're really providing is the illusion of wealth, a parade of flashy purchases that scream, "Look at me!" You drive cars you can't afford, wear watches you don't need, and blow money on gadgets and clothes that serve no purpose other than reinforcing the façade. Budgeting? That's a foreign concept. Savings accounts? For the weak. Instead, you pour your resources into risky investments like crypto scams and then act shocked when the house of cards collapses. You call yourself a provider, but the only thing you consistently deliver is a mountain of bad financial decisions.

This performative economics game doesn't just hurt you, it fuels a whole industry of exploitation and excess. Your relentless need to appear wealthy props up predatory lending, fast fashion, and all the hollow markers of consumer culture. And when the pressure becomes too much, you start pointing fingers. It's not your fault you're drowning in debt, it's society's fault for not rewarding your hustle. It's women's fault for being too independent. It's cancel culture's fault for ruining your entrepreneurial dreams. You refuse to see the truth: you're not a victim of external forces. You're a victim of your own choices, your own refusal to question the myths you've built your life around.

But the grind doesn't stop, does it? Every gym selfie, every podcast rant, every overpriced gadget you buy is just another Band-Aid slapped over the gaping wound of your self-doubt. You tell yourself you're winning, but deep down, you know the truth: the grind isn't empowering you. It's trapping you. You're stuck in a loop of performative success, chasing validation but never catching it. And the harder you try to convince yourself, and everyone else, that you're thriving, the more obvious it becomes that you're not. Your life has become a performance, and the audience isn't buying it.

This is the paradox of your alpha identity: the very things you think will bring you power are the ones that expose your greatest weaknesses. Your interruptions don't show dominance; they reveal fear. Your flashy spending doesn't prove success; it highlights insecurity. Your relentless grind doesn't make you stronger; it wears you down. And the ideals of masculinity you cling to? They're outdated myths, trapping you in a cycle of frustration and failure.

And this is why we laugh, not out of cruelty, but because the contradictions of your life are too absurd to ignore. You preach dominance while living in fear of being irrelevant. You demand respect without earning it. You build your identity around a fantasy of power, only to discover that dominance isn't what you thought it was. The alpha apocalypse isn't the rise of a new masculine ideal, it's the slow, spectacular collapse of an old one. It's a bad reality show you can't turn off, starring you and your overpriced watch in the silence of your empty victories.

Will you learn from your mistakes? Probably not. But at least the rest of us can enjoy the spectacle. Welcome to the grindset. May your interruptions echo and your credit score endure as you continue chasing the mirage of alpha success. Bravo. Take a bow. You've earned it.

Feel Free to Draw a Picture of Your Self Emasculation Below

Chapter 2
Broconomics
Why You're Still Broke

The Blame Economy

Your relationship with the economy is, in a word, tragicomic. If someone asks why you're broke, you'll roll out an entire buffet of excuses, ranging from mildly absurd to outright delusional. Feminists, of course, are your go-to scapegoats, because who else could possibly be responsible for the fact that you can't pay your rent? Right behind them are socialism (which you define as any form of government regulation), avocado toast (still inexplicably blamed for millennial poverty), and the ever-nebulous specter of "cancel culture." The sheer creativity of your grievances might be impressive if it weren't so transparently ridiculous. Somehow, you've convinced yourself that your financial woes have nothing to do with your decisions and everything to do with external forces conspiring against you. It's a masterclass in deflection, wrapped in the flimsiest veneer of logic, and it would almost be funny if it weren't so painfully predictable.

At the heart of your economic worldview lies an undying reverence for the free market. For you, capitalism isn't just a system, it's a religion. You worship at the altar of the "grind," preaching that hard work and hustle will inevitably lead to riches. But this isn't capitalism as Adam Smith envisioned it; it's capitalism reimagined by Instagram influencers and TikTok bros. For you, it's all about the aesthetics of wealth, flashy cars, designer watches, and luxury vacations, without any of the unglamorous groundwork that real financial success requires. The grind is your identity, a badge of honor signifying your commitment to a dream that, for most, will never materialize. You fetishize stories of self-made billionaires while ignoring the systemic advantages that often underpin those success stories.

You celebrate deregulation and tax cuts for the wealthy, blissfully unaware that these policies do nothing for your own bank account. And you chant mantras about personal responsibility while failing to take responsibility for your financial choices. The irony is palpable: your devotion to capitalism blinds you to its flaws, and your refusal to engage with nuance ensures you remain stuck in a cycle of self-inflicted financial ruin.

When things inevitably go wrong, and they always do, you turn to your favorite pastime: finger-pointing. Every maxed-out credit card, every late rent payment, every failed business venture becomes an opportunity for you to rail against "the system." You blame feminists for disrupting the traditional family structure, as though a stable nuclear family could magically erase your reckless spending habits. You blame socialism, which you seem to define as anything that doesn't directly benefit you, for stifling your entrepreneurial spirit. You blame "cancel culture" for creating a hostile business environment, even though your ventures usually fail due to poor planning, not public backlash. And when all else fails, you invoke the ominous specter of "the matriarchy." In your mind, women wield some shadowy power that sabotages you at every turn. Never mind that women are disproportionately affected by economic inequality, if your life is hard, it must be because women are taking too much.

The most laughable part of your finger-pointing is your sheer lack of self-awareness. You rant about "the system" as though it's some abstract, external force completely divorced from your own actions. But here's the truth: you're complicit in perpetuating the very systems you claim to despise. You cheer for deregulation, then act surprised when corporations exploit you. You dismiss calls for a living wage, then complain about your own financial struggles. You glorify hyper-individualism, then wonder why no one rushes to bail you out when you fall on hard times. It's a vicious cycle of self-sabotage, fueled by your refusal to acknowledge reality. Instead of breaking the cycle, you double down on your grievances, shouting louder into the void as if volume alone could solve your problems.

The comedic irony of your grievances is impossible to ignore. You're furious with the economy while actively participating in practices that keep you broke. You idolize capitalism but refuse to engage with its most basic principles, like budgeting or long-term planning. You rail against systemic inequality but dismiss any attempts to address it as "socialism." You claim to be a self-made man, yet you spend half your time blaming everyone else for your failures. Your approach to economics is a perfect microcosm of your larger worldview: performative, contradictory, and ultimately self-defeating.

But perhaps the greatest irony is that your complaints, as absurd as they are, contain a kernel of truth. Yes, the economic system is flawed. Yes, systemic inequality exists. Yes, the playing field is tilted in favor of the wealthy and powerful. But instead of engaging with these issues in a meaningful way, you retreat into your echo chamber, spinning conspiracy theories and lashing out at imaginary enemies. You could be advocating for policies that would benefit everyone, universal healthcare, affordable housing, fair wages, but that would require admitting your rugged individualism isn't enough. So you stay stuck, clinging to your delusions and blaming the world for your woes.

In the end, your approach to economics is as unsustainable as it is laughable. Your fixation on external blame ensures you never address the real causes of your problems, and your refusal to engage with reality keeps you trapped in a cycle of financial instability. It's a tragicomedy of epic proportions, where the joke is always on you, and you're too busy shouting about avocado toast to notice. Welcome to the blame economy. Pull up a chair, because this show isn't ending anytime soon.

Investments in Absurdity

Your relationship with the economy is, in a word, tragicomic. When traditional pathways to financial stability, education, steady employment, sound investments, fail to deliver the instant gratification you crave, you turn to speculative assets and schemes so absurd that even the faintest whiff of due diligence would send most people running. But not you. No, you're convinced that your fortune lies in NFTs, crypto tokens with cartoon dog mascots, and an endless carousel of get-rich-quick fantasies. The irony, of course, is that the only people getting rich are the ones selling these schemes, but you don't want to hear that, you're too busy buying another JPEG of a monkey in sunglasses to listen.

Let's start with NFTs and crypto catastrophes, the crown jewels of your "investment" strategy. Sure, Bitcoin has its decentralized merits, but the cryptocurrencies you champion are little more than glorified Ponzi schemes wrapped in slick branding. You pin your hopes on meme coins and unregulated exchanges, treating your investments like lottery tickets instead of financial strategies. The allure is obvious: in a world where grinding away at a traditional job feels soul-crushing, the promise of making millions overnight is intoxicating. But reality? Far less glamorous. Market crashes wipe out your portfolio faster than you can shout, "To the moon!" Yet, even as your digital fortune evaporates, you double down, convinced the next coin or NFT drop will be the one to turn your life around. It's the financial equivalent of throwing money into a wishing well, except the well is on fire, and you're the one who lit it.

If speculative assets are your lottery tickets, then multi-level marketing schemes are your scratch cards: cheap, addictive, and almost guaranteed to disappoint. MLMs thrive on your desperation and your dreams of financial independence. From dubious testosterone-boosting supplements to workshops on becoming a "self-made alpha," these schemes offer you the illusion of success that's as hollow as the promises they sell. The pitch is always the same: buy in, recruit others, and watch the money roll in. But the reality is a pyramid of broken dreams, with you stuck at the bottom while those at the top rake in the profits. Still, you cling to these schemes, convinced that the only reason you haven't succeeded is that you haven't tried hard enough. It's a perfect microcosm of your worldview: failure isn't the fault of the system, it's a personal shortcoming that you can only overcome by grinding harder.

And then there's the Lamborghini delusion, your fixation on unattainable status symbols. For you, wealth isn't about financial security or building generational stability, it's about flexing. Luxury cars, designer watches, and branded suits aren't things you buy because they add value to your life. You want them because they scream dominance. The Lamborghini is more than a car to you; it's a trophy, a physical manifestation of the alpha lifestyle you aspire to. Never mind that you can't afford the payments. Never mind that the car depreciates faster than your crypto wallet. The point isn't to own something of worth, the point is to be seen as owning it. So you max out your credit cards, take out predatory loans, and post endlessly on social media about the grind that got you "here," even if "here" is a rented sports car you'll return tomorrow.

But let's not pretend that these spending habits are driven by ambition, they're driven by insecurity. You thrive on competition, pitting yourself against others in an endless game of one-upmanship. The economics of envy fuel your every decision, pushing you to spend money you don't have on things you don't need to impress people who aren't even paying attention. It's not about what you want, it's about what you think you need to prove your worth. And the result? A cycle of financial self-destruction, where every flex comes with a hidden cost. You work harder to earn more, only to buy things you can't afford, all to mask the nagging sense that none of it is enough. And it never will be, because your spending isn't driven by logic or necessity, it's driven by a desperate need to validate your fragile ego.

In the end, your investments in absurdity aren't just financial blunders, they're symptoms of something deeper. You're not just chasing wealth; you're chasing identity, validation, and a sense of purpose in a world that no longer caters to your outdated ideals. But instead of addressing the root causes of your dissatisfaction, you throw money at distractions, hoping that the next big thing will finally fill the void. It won't, of course, but that won't stop you from trying. After all, the grind never stops, and neither does the absurdity.

The Whining Economy

If there's one thing you've perfected, it's the art of whining. Complaints are your true currency, endlessly exchanged across podcasts, forums, and TikTok rants. You don't produce solutions, you produce grievances, wrapped in buzzwords and drenched in self-pity. For you, whining isn't just a habit; it's a lifestyle. It's your version of a side hustle, a way to stay relevant in a world that increasingly ignores you. Every failed investment, every botched crypto scheme, every maxed-out credit card becomes fodder for another long-winded tirade about how "the system" is rigged against you. But the irony is that these complaints, while loud and persistent, accomplish nothing except to highlight your own inability to adapt. Whining isn't power, it's the last refuge of someone who's run out of ideas.

And then there's your reliance on the self-help industrial complex, which feeds you a steady diet of toxic advice disguised as wisdom. You flock to self-proclaimed financial gurus who peddle vague platitudes and sketchy investment strategies as the keys to success. "Manifest your wealth!" they shout, conveniently glossing over the fact that manifesting doesn't pay the bills. "Hustle harder!" they demand, as though exhaustion is a substitute for financial literacy. These gurus are the high priests of Broconomics, promising salvation through relentless grind and risky ventures. Their advice rarely amounts to more than empty rhetoric: work harder, buy their course, and don't ask questions. And you, desperate for answers, lap it up, even as your bank account dwindles and your life falls further into chaos. It's a vicious cycle, with the gurus growing richer while you sink deeper into financial despair.

The true irony of your Broconomics lies in its contradictions. You worship capitalism, holding it up as the ultimate arbiter of value and success, yet you're the first to blame it when things don't go your way. You chant the gospel of personal responsibility but refuse to take any when your get-rich-quick schemes inevitably fail. You demand dominance and respect but make decisions that scream desperation and insecurity. You rail against the "rigged system," not realizing, or refusing to acknowledge, that the real problem isn't the system; it's your refusal to adapt. Your financial worldview is a house of cards, built on a foundation of performative masculinity and wishful thinking. And as it collapses, your only response is to shout louder, hoping that someone, somewhere, will take you seriously.

But here's the truth: your whining economy is as unsustainable as your investment strategies. Complaints won't pay the rent, and toxic advice won't fix what's broken. Still, you keep doubling down on the same tactics that got you into trouble in the first place. You're trapped in a feedback loop of failure, clinging to a fantasy that refuses to materialize. And while it's easy to mock your contradictions, and let's be honest, you've earned it, it's also a stark reminder of how deeply flawed your worldview is. If your approach to economics is this doomed, what other aspects of your grindset are equally disastrous? Spoiler alert: it's all of them. But don't worry, we'll get to that in the next chapter.

List of all the things a bad character cannot buy- because some things, no matter how much you spend, aren't for sale:

Respect – Genuine respect is earned, not purchased with flashy cars or overpriced suits.
Integrity – You can't put a price tag on doing the right thing, even when no one is watching.
Love – Relationships built on money are as shallow as the wallet funding them.
Friendship – True friends don't stick around for the private jets, they stay for who you are.
Trust – Once broken, trust can't be bought back, no matter the bribe.
Authenticity – Faking it for the 'gram doesn't make you real.
Wisdom – Reading self-help platitudes isn't the same as understanding life.
Happiness – No amount of Lamborghinis fill the void inside.
Empathy – Caring about others can't be outsourced or purchased in bulk.
Self-awareness – The mirror doesn't sell clarity, no matter how gilded its frame.
Peace of mind – Sleepless nights can't be fixed by luxury bedding.
Purpose – A private island won't give your life meaning.
Grit – True resilience isn't for sale in motivational seminars.
Humility – No amount of bling can mask arrogance.
Kindness – Charity for clout doesn't count.
Redemption – Apologies mean more than throwing money at a problem.
Time – The one currency no one can replenish.
Simplicity – Complicated lives can't buy simplicity back.
Family – Estranged relatives can't be wooed with bank transfers.
Legacy – History remembers character, not net worth.

Feel Free to Draw a Picture of Your 'Real' Lamborghini Below

Chapter 3
Fitness & Fiascos
Get Jacked or Get Judged

The Gym as Therapy for the Emotionally Stunted

The gym isn't just where you work out, it's where you hide. You call it therapy, but let's be honest: it's not about addressing your feelings, it's about bench-pressing them into submission. You're not lifting to be healthy or balanced; you're lifting to prove something, either to yourself or to some imagined audience. Your emotional trauma? That's what the dumbbells are for. Feeling insecure about your relationships or your place in the world? Just crank out some deadlifts and convince yourself that everything's fine. Need to process the fact that you don't actually like the guy staring back at you in the mirror? No need. Just flex harder, slap on some protein shake bravado, and post a selfie with a motivational caption about grinding. Because in your world, "looking strong" is the same as "being strong," and who needs feelings when you've got gains?

But here's the problem: the gym isn't a therapist's office, no matter how many hours you spend there or how many pounds you can lift. All those reps and sets won't solve your deeper issues. You're trading emotional intelligence for physical strength, as if bulging biceps can fill the gaping hole where your self-awareness should be. Sure, you might look like you've got it together, but muscles don't make you a man. Real strength isn't about how much weight you can throw around, it's about being able to face your vulnerabilities without running from them. And let's be real: you're not just running from them, you're trying to bury them under a mountain of plates. You've convinced yourself that working out is the solution to everything, but in reality, it's just a distraction. You're channeling all that energy into building a body that you think will protect you, but no matter how big your shoulders get, they're not going to carry the emotional baggage you refuse to unpack.

What makes it worse is how the culture of toxic masculinity thrives in gym spaces. You don't just lift weights; you lift the entire weight of macho posturing and grindset culture. It's not enough to work out, you have to buy into the entire lifestyle. That means drowning yourself in protein shakes, popping pre-workout pills, and loading up on every supplement that promises to make you bigger, faster, stronger. Never mind the fact that you're probably sacrificing your long-term health for short-term aesthetics. And then there's the steroids. Sure, you justify it by saying "everyone's doing it," but deep down, you know it's just another way to shortcut the hard work of becoming a better person. You're not building character; you're building a façade, one that you hope will make people overlook everything else you're not.

But the gym isn't just about physical strength, is it? It's also where you go to perform. Everything about your time there screams performative masculinity. From the way you grunt louder than necessary to the endless selfies in front of the mirror, it's clear that this isn't about health or self-improvement, it's about validation. You post those gym photos with captions like "No pain, no gain," as if that's supposed to mean something profound. But let's be honest, you're not sharing those pictures to inspire anyone. You're sharing them because you need people to see you, to validate you, to tell you that all this effort is worth something. And maybe for a moment, it feels like it is. But those likes and comments aren't going to fill the void. They're just temporary fixes, like a sugar rush that leaves you crashing harder than before.

And then there's the way you prioritize appearance over substance. Take leg day, for example. You skip it because, let's face it, nobody's looking at your legs. You focus on the muscles that are easiest to show off, your chest, your arms, your abs, because those are the ones that get you attention. But in doing so, you're missing the bigger picture. Just like in life, ignoring the foundational stuff is going to catch up with you. Sure, you might look great in a tank top, but without balance, you're just setting yourself up for problems down the road. And it's not just your physical foundation you're neglecting. It's your emotional foundation too. You're so busy trying to look the part of the "alpha male" that you've completely neglected the work it takes to actually *be* strong, mentally, emotionally, and socially.

What you don't seem to realize is that this obsession with dominance, with performing strength, is exactly what's holding you back. The gym has become a symbol of your refusal to confront reality. You've built a temple to yourself, but it's a hollow one, filled with insecurities that you've dressed up as confidence. The saddest part? It doesn't have to be this way. You could use the gym as a tool for genuine growth, not just physically, but emotionally. You could let it be a space where you challenge yourself, not just to lift heavier weights but to confront the things you're running from. But instead, you've turned it into a place where you hide, where you feed into a culture that values appearances over substance and noise over introspection.

So, where does that leave you? You've got the body you always wanted, but you're still carrying the same emotional baggage you had when you started. You've built a life around looking strong, but deep down, you know the truth: you're not. Real strength isn't about muscles or how much weight you can lift. It's about facing the things that scare you, that challenge you, that force you to grow. And until you're willing to do that, no amount of protein shakes, gym selfies, or personal bests is going to make you the man you want to be. The gym might be where you work out, but it's also where you've been working hardest to avoid yourself. Maybe it's time to stop running and start lifting the things that actually matter.

Performative Fitness and the Social Media Machine

The gym isn't just where you go to work out anymore, it's where you stage your performance. And what's a performance without an audience? Enter the gym selfie, the cornerstone of your online identity. Every session becomes an opportunity to broadcast your "dedication" to the world. It's not enough to lift; you have to document it. You strike a pose in front of the mirror, flexing just right to catch the lighting, and post it with captions like "No pain, no gain!" or "Alpha mode activated!" as if that's supposed to convince anyone you're living your best life. But let's be honest: the gym selfie isn't about fitness. It's about validation. You don't really care if you're inspiring others; you care about the likes, the comments, the digital applause that tells you all those hours in the gym mean something.

What you don't realize is how isolating this obsession with performative fitness has made you. You've traded meaningful connections for followers and family dinners for workouts. Friends don't call anymore, probably because they're tired of hearing about your max bench press or your latest PR. And when they do reach out, you're too busy chasing gains to notice. Your social life isn't built around shared experiences or mutual care, it's built around your curated online persona. You think the gym makes you stronger, but it's pulling you further away from the relationships that could actually support you. Your followers might admire your abs, but they don't know you. And deep down, you know they don't care.

But it's not just the isolation that's the problem. It's the way you prioritize looking strong over actually being healthy. You're so focused on building the perfect body that you've ignored what it's costing you. Burnout, injuries, and exhaustion are all par for the course when you're chasing an aesthetic instead of a balanced lifestyle. You tell yourself that the pain is worth it because it proves how tough you are, but what you're really doing is ignoring the warning signs that your body, and your mind, are giving you. Strength isn't just about muscles; it's about resilience, adaptability, and balance. And right now, you're trading all of that for a six-pack and a highlight reel of gym selfies.

The worst part? The fitness industry loves this mindset because it makes you the perfect customer. They prey on your insecurities, selling you overpriced supplements that promise gains but deliver little more than an empty wallet. You shell out for bogus workout plans designed to keep you coming back for more, and you chase unattainable body ideals promoted by influencers who are either genetically blessed, chemically enhanced, or both. The entire industry is built on your desperation to look the part of the alpha male while ignoring the things that really matter, like health, sustainability, and self-worth. It's not about making you stronger; it's about making you spend more.

So here you are, stuck in a cycle of performative fitness. You work out not because you enjoy it or because it's good for you, but because you think it will prove something, to yourself, to your followers, to the world. But what are you really proving? That you can lift heavy things? That you can spend hours in the gym every week? That you know how to strike a pose? None of that makes you a better person. None of it builds the kind of strength that matters. And until you realize that, you'll keep chasing a version of fitness that leaves you looking good on the outside and empty on the inside. You might have a hundred thousand likes, but what good is that if you're too burned out and disconnected to enjoy it? The gym doesn't have to be a stage. It could be a place of growth, connection, and health. But as long as you're using it to perform, you'll never experience any of that. You'll just keep flexing for an audience that's already moved on to the next post.

The Gains That Don't Matter

You've worked so hard to build your body, chasing those gains with relentless determination, but let's talk about the limits of what all that strength actually means. Sure, you've got bulging biceps, a shredded core, and maybe even some decent shoulders, but what else? Does it make you happy? Does it bring you closer to the people who matter in your life? Does it give you the tools to handle conflict, communicate effectively, or find meaning in your relationships? No? Then what's the point? Physical fitness alone doesn't equate to well-being. You've prioritized aesthetics over substance, muscles over mindfulness, and now you're left with the nagging emptiness of having reached your superficial goals without addressing anything deeper. You might look strong, but strength isn't just about your ability to lift weights, it's about resilience, adaptability, and emotional stability. Without those, your gains don't matter.

Let's talk about expectations. The manosphere has convinced you that real men need to embody hypermasculine ideals, including an impossible level of physical perfection. You're supposed to be jacked, ripped, and ready to dominate. But what they don't tell you is how unsustainable that is. The constant grind to achieve and maintain these unrealistic standards takes a toll, on your body, your mind, and your sense of self. You've bought into a fantasy, and it's costing you. The reality is, nobody can be at their peak 24/7. Bodies change. Life happens. And when the inevitable occurs, an injury, a missed workout, or just the passage of time, you're left grappling with a crisis of identity because you've tied your self-worth to something so fleeting.

The saddest part is how perfectly your gym habits reflect your broader worldview. Just like your fitness routine, your life is short-sighted and surface-level. You focus on the things that are easiest to measure, how much you can lift, how shredded you look, while ignoring the deeper issues that require real work. You'd rather flex in the mirror than take a hard look at yourself. You'd rather push through another set than address why you're so angry, bitter, or lonely. The gym isn't just where you work out; it's a metaphor for how you approach everything. You're so focused on appearing strong that you've forgotten what it means to actually *be* strong. Real strength isn't loud, performative, or superficial. It's quiet, steady, and built on a foundation of self-awareness and integrity, two things you've been avoiding.

So, where does that leave you? You've spent all this time chasing gains that don't matter, and for what? To look dominant? To feel better than others? To convince yourself you're in control? The truth is, your obsession with appearing strong mirrors your obsession with dominance in every other area of life. You've built yourself up physically, but emotionally and mentally, you're still skipping the hard work. You haven't built a foundation; you've built a façade. And just like the gym selfies you're so proud of, it's all surface-level, hollow and fleeting.

As we move into the next chapter, consider this: Strength isn't about how you look or what you can lift, it's about what you're willing to face. Right now, you're running from everything that actually matters. But don't worry, we'll keep watching, and yes, we'll keep laughing, because nothing is funnier than someone who thinks they've got it all figured out while avoiding the things that truly count. Stay tuned.

Feel Free to Draw a Tiny Picture of Your Tiny Legs Below

Chapter 4
The Red Pill Diet
Swallowing Patriarchy Whole

What's in the Red Pill

The gym has become your unofficial therapist's office, a sacred refuge where your emotions are benched right alongside the barbells. But let's be real, it's not about addressing your feelings or unpacking your trauma. It's about lifting heavy things until the world starts making sense. If it ever does. For you, the gym isn't just a place to get fit; it's a shrine to the idea that brute force can somehow fix what's broken inside. Why talk about your feelings when you can drown them out with the clanging of weights and the endless droning of bro podcasts blasting in your AirPods? The gym becomes your theater of repression, where every rep and every drop of sweat screams, "I'm fine!" while your inner turmoil quietly curls up in the corner, waiting for attention you'll never give it.

Working out isn't just exercise for you, it's an escape route. You've turned fitness into a coping mechanism to avoid emotional growth. Why grapple with the complexities of vulnerability or self-awareness when you can flex in front of a mirror and convince yourself that your worth lies in the size of your arms? You genuinely believe that bulging biceps and shredded abs can compensate for a glaring lack of emotional intelligence. Forget working on your personality or addressing those daddy issues, just add more plates to the barbell, bro. Your culture of fitness defines strength solely by appearance, masking emotional weakness with physical muscle, and avoids vulnerability at all costs. This isn't self-improvement; it's self-delusion, served with a protein shake chaser.

Speaking of protein shakes, let's talk about the toxic brew that fuels your vision of masculinity. Gym spaces thrive on a cocktail of protein powders, pre-workout stimulants, and anabolic steroids, all marketed as the keys to dominance. Forget health, this isn't about living longer or feeling better. It's about looking like a Marvel superhero, no matter the cost to your liver or your sanity. Add in the endless gym jargon, "beast mode," "alpha gains," and "no excuses," and you've got a recipe for a deeply unhealthy relationship with fitness. Instead of promoting balance and well-being, you've turned the gym into a breeding ground for toxic ideals, where strength is measured by how much you can lift and masculinity is defined by how intimidating you look.

And let's not ignore the tragic phenomenon of skipping leg day. Nothing reveals the performative nature of your fitness culture quite like this. Why bother working on the muscles that don't get noticed in a mirror selfie? Your focus is always on the show muscles, the biceps, the chest, the abs, while your legs are left to languish in obscurity. It's a perfect metaphor for your broader approach to life: focus on appearances, ignore the foundations. You'll spend hours sculpting your upper body while your legs remain comically underdeveloped, a literal representation of your imbalanced priorities. Who needs stability and strength when your pecs can practically wink at you?

In the end, the gym isn't therapy for you. It's a stage, a place where you can pretend you've got your life together by lifting heavy things and glaring at your reflection. It's where you escape your insecurities by building the illusion of strength while avoiding the hard work of actual self-improvement. So, the next time you're flexing in the mirror after skipping leg day, remember this: you're not just working out your body, you're running away from your feelings. And no amount of protein powder can fix that.

Building an Identity on Fragility

Red pill ideology is, at its core, a placebo, an emotional sugar pill that promises you enlightenment and empowerment but delivers nothing more than the illusion of control. When you swallow it, you convince yourself you've uncovered some grand, hidden truth about society, but what you've really found is a well-packaged excuse for your anger and resentment. Instead of solving your problems, the red pill traps you in cycles of frustration, bitterness, and blame. It offers you a distorted lens to view the world, one that reinforces your insecurities and tells you that your failures aren't your fault. The result? A self-reinforcing loop of superiority complexes masking deep-seated inferiority. You think you're mastering the game, but you're really just playing along without understanding the rules.

The genius, and tragedy, of red pill culture lies in how it turns your fragility into a lifestyle. Everything becomes a challenge to your masculinity. Did a woman disagree with you in a meeting? Clearly, she's part of the feminist agenda. Did a bartender serve your drink with a pink straw? A deliberate attack on your alpha status. Did you lose a job, fail to get a second date, or feel excluded from a social circle? It must be society's obsession with emasculating men, not your own inability to connect or contribute meaningfully. The red pill demands that you see threats everywhere and respond with over-the-top bravado, turning everyday interactions into exhausting battles for dominance. You're so busy proving your strength that you don't notice how brittle you've become, snapping under the slightest pressure.

What's worse is how red pill ideology encourages you to disguise your personality problems as oppression. You refuse to take responsibility for your own behavior, choosing instead to blame feminism, "the matriarchy," or modern dating culture. If you're rude or dismissive to a woman and she doesn't want to date you, it's not because of your actions, it's because women are "too picky" or "don't appreciate a good man." If you lack emotional intelligence or self-awareness, it's not your fault, it's because society doesn't value traditional masculinity anymore. This relentless externalization of blame creates a worldview where you're always the victim and never the problem. It's a neat little trick that allows you to avoid introspection entirely, but it's also the reason you never grow or change.

Your emotional fragility is like outdated software, buggy, clunky, and in desperate need of an update. Imagine a computer program that hasn't been patched in decades, still running on 1990s logic and unable to process modern realities. That's red pill masculinity in a nutshell. Instead of fixing the bugs, you double down on the faulty code, refusing to adapt because you believe the problem isn't your system, it's everyone else's. You cling to outdated ideas about gender roles, relationships, and success, convinced that if you yell "facts don't care about your feelings" loudly enough, you'll win. But the only thing you're winning is a race to the bottom, alienating everyone around you while insisting you're the one who's figured it all out.

The tragic comedy of it all becomes obvious the moment you open your mouth. You'll spend hours ranting about how men are supposed to be stoic, strong, and unshakable, yet you crumble at the mere suggestion that your worldview might be flawed. A woman orders a latte? An existential crisis. A man wears sunscreen? Proof that society has gone soft. A TV show features a female lead? Evidence of the impending collapse of Western civilization. Your inability to handle even the smallest perceived challenge to your masculinity reveals just how precarious your sense of self truly is. You're not an alpha, you're a paper tiger, roaring loudly to hide how easily you tear.

Red pill ideology doesn't empower you; it shackles you. It gives you permission to avoid self-reflection, excuses your worst impulses, and keeps you locked in a cycle of bitterness and blame. You think you've swallowed a path to enlightenment, but all you've really done is drink the Kool-Aid of toxic masculinity, trading growth for grievance. You're not building an identity, you're building a cage, one bar of insecurity at a time. And instead of breaking free, you keep reinforcing the walls, convincing yourself that the problem is out there, when it's been within you all along.

Patriarchy Isn't the Answer

Red pill ideology serves up patriarchy as the ultimate solution, an elixir of control, dominance, and order that promises to fix what ails you, the modern man. But swallowing patriarchy whole is like chugging expired medicine, it doesn't cure the sickness; it deepens it. These outdated and harmful norms might have provided a false sense of structure in another era, but in today's world, they're an anchor, dragging you further from meaningful relationships and personal growth. The red pill convinces you that returning to "traditional" gender roles will restore balance, but in reality, it isolates you. Clinging to these ideas in a world that has moved forward isn't just impractical, it's self-destructive. Instead of finding connection and fulfillment, you end up alone, shouting into an echo chamber that grows smaller with each passing day.

The cost of this ideology is steep. At its core, red pill thinking demands that you reject vulnerability, empathy, and emotional intelligence, all the things that make relationships meaningful. Instead, it tells you to double down on control, to view women as adversaries or prizes rather than partners, and to measure success through superficial markers of dominance. The result? Toxic relationships marked by resentment and dysfunction. You sabotage connections before they can deepen, dismiss kindness as weakness, and trade potential happiness for performative strength. And when these relationships inevitably fail, you chalk it up to external forces, feminism, the "matriarchy," modernity, rather than examining your own behavior. Self-improvement isn't just overlooked; it's actively discouraged, replaced by an endless loop of grievance and deflection.

The irony of red pill ideology is that it promises enlightenment but delivers nothing more than a well-decorated prison cell for your fragile ego. It markets itself as a path to truth, but its truths are cherry-picked, simplistic, and often outright false. The supposed insights of the red pill, about relationships, gender dynamics, and power, aren't revelations; they're repackaged clichés that crumble under scrutiny. It doesn't empower you; it insulates you, wrapping you in layers of anger, fear, and blame until you can't see the world beyond your own insecurities. This isn't a path to freedom, it's a detour into a self-imposed echo chamber where the same tired grievances are repeated ad nauseam, each iteration more disconnected from reality than the last.

And yet, the allure of the red pill persists, not because it delivers on its promises, but because it absolves you of responsibility. It tells you what you want to hear: that your problems aren't your fault, that society has betrayed you, and that you are the true victim. It gives you a community, even if that community is built on shared resentment rather than genuine connection. It's comforting in the way that all lies are comforting, easy to accept, difficult to confront. But the comfort is fleeting, and the consequences are long-lasting.

As this chapter closes, it's impossible not to laugh at the absurdity of the red pill's central conceit: turning fragility into a brand. It markets weakness as strength, bitterness as wisdom, and fear as enlightenment. The red pill doesn't challenge you to grow; it coddles you, feeding your insecurities while pretending to build you up. And as you sit in your echo chamber, sipping on your bile and blaming the world, you miss the bigger picture entirely. So laugh, if you can, at the absurdity of it all. Because while the red pill might offer you a distorted view of reality, the real joke is how thoroughly you've bought into it.

PS: Meeting Your Heroes, Oops, Bro

Ah, the red pill, a symbol you've proudly co-opted from *The Matrix* movies, waving it like a banner of supposed enlightenment. But here's the kicker: the metaphor you clutch so dearly wasn't the brainchild of some hyper-masculine prophets of dominance. It was created by the Wachowski siblings, who are now the Wachowski sisters. That's right, the creators of your sacred metaphor transitioned genders and have since shared that *The Matrix* was deeply inspired by themes of identity, self-discovery, and the fluidity of gender. Turns out, the red pill wasn't a shortcut to dominance; it was a gateway to exploring truths you'd rather not confront.

The original red pill wasn't about battling feminism or dodging accountability, it was a call to awaken to the complexities of self and society, to embrace transformation in all its messy, human glory. While you've twisted it into a tool for clinging to outdated norms, its creators envisioned it as a celebration of liberation and authenticity. The irony? The metaphor you've weaponized against change was born from a story of radical acceptance and courage. Meeting your heroes doesn't always go as planned, does it? But don't worry, you can always scuttle back to your echo chamber and pretend this inconvenient truth doesn't exist.

So, the joke is on you. HA HA HA HA HA HA!!!

Yes, yes, we are laughing at you, because you are a laughingstock. And now, perhaps it's time to take stock of yourselves and grow up before you ruin absolutely everything on land, air, sea, and even space. Oh, but don't stress too much about your place in the cosmos; your beloved tech philosopher-kings don't care about you either. They're too busy compensating for their own insecurities with phallic-shaped rockets, desperately trying to fill their hollow, phallic-thropic yearnings and glaring inadequacies. The joke, as always, is on you.

Alternatives to Swallowing the Red Pill

Go to Therapy – Instead of blaming society for your problems, talk to a professional who can help you unpack your feelings and build healthier ways of thinking. Spoiler: It's not weak; it's smart.

Read Books by Women – Expand your worldview with authors like bell hooks or Roxane Gay. You might just learn something that doesn't involve "alpha" or "beta."

Practice Active Listening – Instead of waiting for your turn to talk, actually hear what others are saying. It's shocking how much you can learn by not interrupting.

Get a Hobby That Isn't About Impressing Others – Find joy in something for its own sake, like gardening, painting, or learning a new skill. It's called growth.

Try Empathy – Imagine how someone else feels instead of making everything about you. It's a stretch, but it's worth it.

Take a Class on Gender Studies – Before ranting about "feminism," understand what it actually means. Education is power.

Build Friendships Without Competition – Not everything has to be a pissing contest. Real connection happens when you drop the "alpha" act.

Volunteer – Helping others reminds you the world isn't just about your struggles. Plus, it's genuinely rewarding.

Laugh at Yourself – Instead of taking life so seriously, learn to joke about your flaws. Self-awareness is attractive.

Ditch the Echo Chamber – Step out of your Red Pill forums and engage with diverse perspectives. Growth happens when you challenge your own beliefs.

Cultivate Emotional Intelligence – Read up on emotional awareness and learn to express your feelings instead of burying them. It's not just for "betas."

Spend Time with Kids or Elders – They'll remind you of what truly matters: connection, perspective, and the simplicity of being present.

Redefine Success – Stop chasing dominance and start focusing on fulfillment. Success isn't about beating others; it's about finding your own purpose.

Feel Free to Draw a Picture of Yourself as a Woman Below

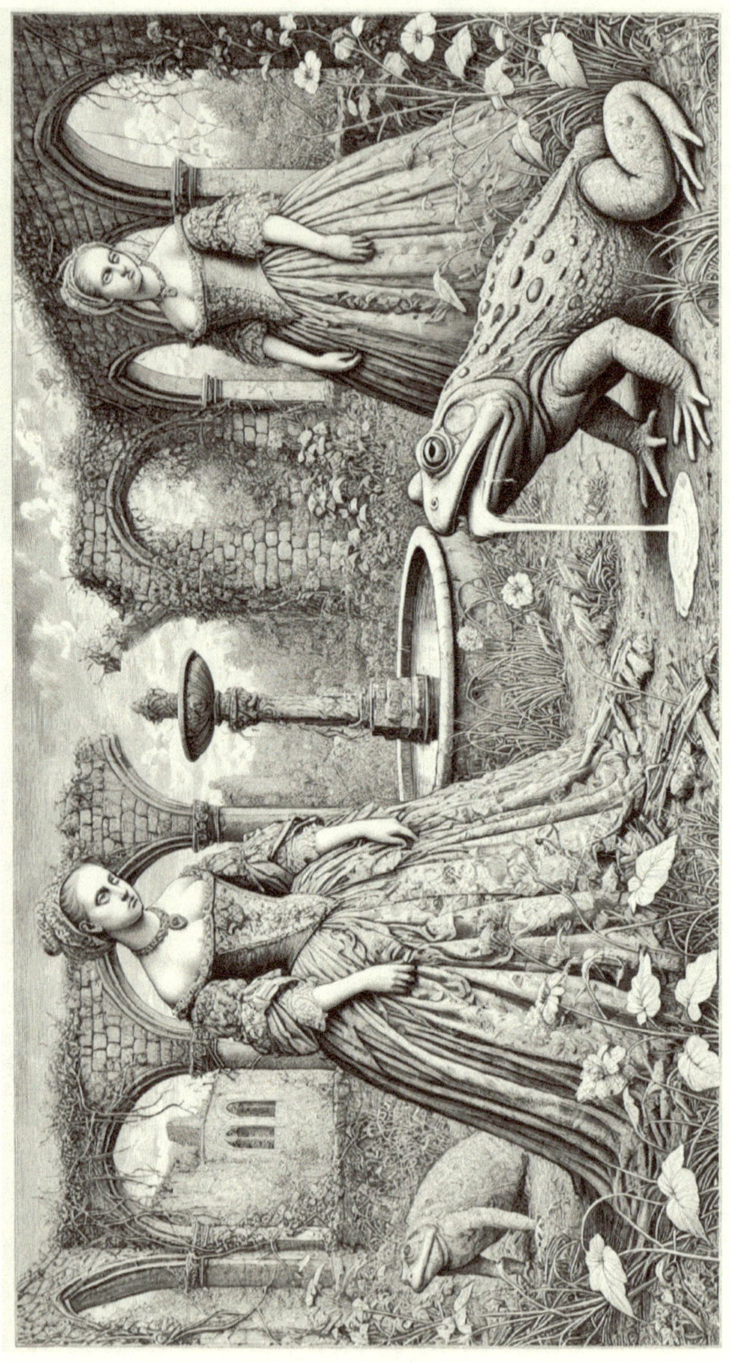

Chapter 5
A Douche is Not Just for Lady Parts
Dating in a Post Feminist Wasteland

Why Are You Still Single?
Dating in a post-feminist wasteland should be a breeze, right? Women have no autonomy, society supposedly tilts in your favor, and you've reclaimed the dominance you were always yammering about. So why, dear bros, are you still single? It's a question worth asking, though you probably won't like the answer. With the playing field entirely rigged in your favor, the problem clearly isn't external. Could it be, brace yourself, that the issue lies within? Maybe it's the way your idea of flirting involves negging women into submission or your assumption that women are puzzles to solve rather than people to engage with. Perhaps it's your dating app bio, which reads less like an invitation to connect and more like a list of red flags set to music. Whatever the reason, it's clear that the supposed "return" to traditional gender roles hasn't fixed your dating woes. If anything, it's just highlighted them in sharper relief.

Let's unpack the manosphere's approach to dating, where relationships aren't seen as mutual endeavors but as zero-sum games. Winning means control, and control means ensuring that your partner knows her place, preferably somewhere below you, emotionally, intellectually, and financially. This mindset turns every interaction into a battlefield, where vulnerability is seen as weakness and dominance is the only currency. Forget connecting over shared interests or engaging in meaningful conversations. Instead, you're out here delivering backhanded compliments (negging) like, "You're pretty for someone who doesn't wear makeup" or "You're smart for a girl." These tactics, borrowed from the dusty playbooks of pick-up artists who peaked in 2006, aren't charming. They're transparent, insulting, and a surefire way to ensure you remain perpetually single.

But the cringeworthy tactics don't stop at negging. Oh no, they extend to your entire dating strategy, especially online. Let's take a moment to examine the manosphere's typical dating app profile. First, the gym selfies. Not just one or two to show you're active, but a full catalog of mirror shots with your face conveniently cropped out to spotlight your abs. Because nothing says "emotionally available" like commodifying your own body. Then there's the bio, a manifesto of misplaced entitlement: "I'm an alpha male looking for a submissive woman who knows how to cook and doesn't talk too much." Charming. And let's not forget the demands: no single moms, no feminists, no drama. Translation? "I want a perfect human being who tolerates my mediocrity."

And let's not forget the bitterness that seeps through in every word. A classic manosphere profile might include phrases like, "Tired of women who can't appreciate a good man," or "I'm not here to play games." These statements reek of unresolved resentment and do nothing to make you seem appealing. They don't say, "I'm confident and ready for a relationship." They scream, "I've been ghosted a lot, and instead of reflecting on why, I've decided the problem is all women." This approach doesn't inspire curiosity or connection; it inspires pity and an immediate left swipe.

So here we are in a dystopia where women's rights have been stripped away, the manosphere's vision of society has been realized, and yet… your dating prospects are still non-existent. How is this possible? Could it be that no amount of societal restructuring can compensate for a personality that repels rather than attracts? Could it be that treating relationships as a competition, where the goal is to "win" rather than connect, makes you less of a partner and more of a chore? The truth is, no matter how many advantages you believe you have, none of them will help if your approach to dating is rooted in arrogance, insecurity, and disdain.

The irony is delicious, isn't it? In a world you've carefully crafted to stack the deck in your favor, you're still struggling. And it's not because women "don't appreciate a good man." It's because, based on your actions, you're not one. Perhaps it's time to reevaluate, to trade negging for genuine conversation, entitlement for empathy, and bitterness for introspection. Or, you know, don't. After all, the rest of us could use the entertainment.

Men Too Dating Apps and the Dystopian Swipe Scene

The manosphere's dream has materialized: Men Too dating apps, tailor-made for bros like you. Finally, a platform where you can find women who align with your "alpha" worldview. Or so you think. These apps promise to connect you with like-minded individuals who supposedly "get it," creating a perfect storm of traditional values and modern swiping. But the reality? You're not building relationships; you're just building a bigger echo chamber. Your profile isn't unique, it's a carbon copy of every other guy who's convinced he's a misunderstood genius. Let's take a wild guess: your gym selfies dominate the photo lineup, your bio makes vague promises about how you're "an alpha male who won't tolerate drama," and there's probably a list of things you don't want in a woman. Oh, and let's not forget the underlying bitterness seeping through every word. This isn't a dating profile; it's a manifesto of insecurity masquerading as confidence.

But even on these apps, where the odds are supposedly stacked in your favor, you're still getting ghosted. Weird, right? Let me guess, you're chalking it up to women being "too picky" or "not appreciating a good man." But here's the thing: women aren't ghosting you because they can't handle your greatness. They're ghosting you because your behavior practically screams, "Run!" Whether it's the way you monopolize conversations to air your grievances about feminism and modern dating or the constant need to steer every interaction back to how the world has wronged you, you're the problem. Ghosting isn't proof of women's flaws; it's proof that you're exhausting to engage with. Let's be real: why would anyone stick around when your idea of a meaningful connection is a thinly veiled pity party disguised as alpha wisdom?

And then there's your favorite date topic: crypto. Yes, the blockchain. You love to talk about it, on dates, in chats, probably even in your bio. You think you're coming off as a savvy investor, a man with vision, someone who "sees the future." But here's the truth: you're not impressing anyone. Nobody wants to hear about how you "beat the market" or why NFTs are the key to generational wealth while they're trying to enjoy their salad. And if you think pixelated monkey JPEGs are a turn-on, you've already lost the plot. Instead of making you sound smart, your obsession with crypto and grindset culture paints you as someone who's more interested in preaching than connecting. Conversations aren't supposed to be one-sided lectures, but somehow, you've managed to make every interaction feel like a TED Talk nobody asked for.

Let's move on to something even more basic: hygiene. Grooming isn't a suggestion, it's the bare minimum. And yet, here you are, either completely ignoring it or going way overboard. Let's talk about your cologne, for instance. Whether you're spraying yourself with cheap drugstore cologne that smells like a middle school locker room or drowning in an overpriced designer fragrance, the result is the same: suffocation. You might think you're adding a touch of sophistication, but really, you're just choking everyone within a five-foot radius. You can't put perfume on a pig, or in this case, cologne on a bro, and expect it to fix what's underneath. And let's not forget the rest of the package: unironed shirts, poorly fitting jeans, and shoes that have clearly seen better days. You think you're exuding dominance, but what you're really broadcasting is desperation. Your whole look screams, "I'm trying too hard, but I still don't get it."

Your approach to grooming is a microcosm of your larger problem: your inability to grasp what's actually appealing. You treat everything as performative. Your cologne isn't about smelling good; it's about projecting an image. Your gym selfies aren't about being fit; they're about demanding attention. Your entire dating strategy is rooted in the idea that dominance and posturing are attractive, but here's the truth, they're not. Nobody is impressed by your attempt to flex your way through life while neglecting the basics of decency, humility, and self-awareness. Your idea of a "manly man" isn't charming; it's exhausting. And the worst part? You think the problem is everyone else.

Let's go back to the Men Too apps for a moment. These platforms were designed for people like you, men who claim they're tired of the "modern dating crisis." They're supposed to connect you with women who "understand" traditional values. But even in this tailored environment, you're still struggling. You're still getting ghosted, still not finding the relationships you want. Why? Because your entire approach is fundamentally broken. These apps don't create compatibility; they create an echo chamber where your worst habits are amplified. Instead of learning and growing, you double down on everything that's holding you back. You think matching with a woman who shares your worldview will solve your problems, but it won't. Because at the end of the day, it's not about the apps or the women or the system. It's about you.

Here's the truth: the problem isn't modern dating or feminism or the supposed "decline of traditional values." The problem is you. It's the way you approach relationships like a transaction, where you expect women to conform to your demands without offering anything meaningful in return. It's the way you refuse to take responsibility for your failures, blaming everyone and everything but yourself. It's the way you treat grooming, conversation, and self-presentation as optional instead of essential. And until you're willing to address those things, you'll stay exactly where you are: swiping endlessly, wondering why nothing works, and convincing yourself it's all someone else's fault.

But don't worry. You'll keep blaming the apps, society, and women. You'll keep thinking that you're the misunderstood genius in a world that just doesn't get you. And you'll keep wondering why, in a world supposedly built for you, you're still so alone.

Sarcastic Dating Tips and the Hard Truth

So you're struggling in the dating world, even in this dystopian paradise where everything is supposedly rigged in your favor. Don't worry, bro, I've got some advice for you. Let's start with the basics, and I mean really basic, because that seems to be where things go off the rails. First, wear deodorant. Nobody wants to get close to someone who smells like gym socks and regret. Second, try asking her about her interests. Instead of monologuing about your crypto portfolio, maybe, just maybe, find out what she's passionate about. And here's a big one: don't call her a feminist villain just because she has opinions. Engage with her as if she's a person, not an obstacle to conquer.

Now let's talk about therapy. I know, you've probably convinced yourself therapy is for weaklings or "beta males," but hear me out. Therapy could be the thing that saves you from yourself. It's not about fixing your problems overnight; it's about understanding why you behave the way you do. All that anger, insecurity, and bitterness you carry around like a badge of honor? That's not strength, that's unexamined pain. Therapy can help you unpack it, confront it, and move past it. Sure, it's easier to blame women, society, or the world for your problems, but that's not going to get you anywhere. Imagine, for a moment, what it would be like to approach a relationship without dragging all your unresolved baggage into it. Scary, right? But worth it.

And then there's the Nice Guy™ narrative, your favorite fallback when things don't go your way. "I'm such a nice guy, why don't women appreciate me?" Here's the hard truth: you're not nice. You're entitled. Being polite or doing something thoughtful doesn't mean someone owes you their time, attention, or affection. True kindness doesn't come with strings attached, but your version always does. You hold doors open, pay for drinks, or listen to her vent, and then you expect a reward at the end, a date, a kiss, or maybe more. That's not kindness; it's a transaction. Women see through it, and it's why your "nice guy" routine doesn't work. If you're only being nice to get something in return, you're not a good guy, you're just manipulative.

So, let's sum up. Wear deodorant. Listen more than you talk. Get yourself to therapy. Stop treating kindness like a currency you can cash in for affection. And recognize that your struggles in the dating world aren't because women don't appreciate you, they're because your approach is fundamentally flawed. Even in this dystopia built to cater to your every whim, you're still striking out. What does that say about you? If you can't succeed in a world restructured to favor your ideals, maybe the problem isn't society. Maybe it's you.

These same insecurities and toxic behaviors don't just ruin your chances at love, they seep into every corner of your life, poisoning your broader social dynamics and eroding meaningful connections. But don't worry, there's still time to reflect and grow. Or you can keep doubling down, clinging to the comfort of your echo chamber. Either way, the absurdity of it all remains undeniable, and, let's be honest, a little laughable.

Examples of Real Men

Mister Rogers – A beacon of kindness and empathy, showing that real strength lies in compassion.

Keanu Reeves – Humble and generous, he's proof that decency can coexist with success.

Nelson Mandela – A global symbol of resilience and forgiveness, he fought for equality with unyielding courage.

Billy Porter – Bold and unapologetic, he redefines masculinity while advocating for individuality and equality.

David Attenborough – A lifelong environmentalist who inspires the world to protect and cherish the planet.

LeBron James – A sports icon dedicated to uplifting communities and prioritizing family values.

Harvey Milk – A pioneer of LGBTQ+ rights whose bravery changed the course of history.

Dwayne "The Rock" Johnson – A symbol of strength and emotional vulnerability, balancing fame and humility.

James Baldwin – A literary genius who championed truth, justice, and understanding across lines of race and identity.

Malala Yousafzai's Father – A progressive voice supporting education and equality in defiance of societal norms.

Cesar Chavez – A tireless advocate for farmworkers' rights, embodying perseverance and dignity.

Lin-Manuel Miranda – A creative visionary who celebrates heritage and inspires inclusivity through art.

Yo-Yo Ma – A brilliant cellist using music to build cultural bridges and promote global harmony.

Russell Means – An American Indian activist who fought for Native rights and cultural preservation with unrelenting passion.

Ban Ki-moon – A South Korean diplomat and former UN Secretary-General dedicated to global cooperation and peace.

RuPaul Charles – A trailblazing entertainer redefining representation through charisma, uniqueness, nerve, and talent.

Shohei Ohtani – A Japanese baseball player redefining the sport with his exceptional skill and sportsmanship.

Taika Waititi – A Maori filmmaker and actor blending humor with social commentary while uplifting indigenous voices.

Feel Free to Draw a Picture of Your Ideal Man Below

Chapter 6
Manhood Redefined
The Fragility Olympics

The Fragility Olympics – An Introduction
Welcome to the Fragility Olympics, the most exclusive competition no one asked for but many seem determined to win. The rules are simple: take every minor inconvenience, every perceived slight, and every instance of someone else simply existing, and turn it into a full-blown existential crisis about your manhood. Pink drinks? Clearly an attack on your masculinity. Sunscreen? Only "soft" men care about skin cancer. Women having opinions? Don't even get started. The contestants in this game aren't vying for strength or resilience; no, they're competing to see who can be the most easily threatened. It's a race to the bottom, and the prize is a lifetime membership to the club of performative outrage. Congratulations, you're already a frontrunner.

Let's talk about what passes for manhood in this ridiculous spectacle. In the world of the manosphere, being a man isn't about facing challenges with dignity or showing courage in the face of adversity. It's about hyper-vigilance against anything that could be remotely interpreted as "soft" or "feminine." You've redefined masculinity, not as strength or confidence, but as a constant need to prove you're tough, usually to an audience that isn't paying attention. You can't enjoy a fruity cocktail without turning it into a statement about your heterosexuality. You can't apply sunscreen without feeling the need to defend it as a "survival tactic" rather than basic self-care. And if a woman dares to express an opinion that differs from yours? Time to break out the caps lock and launch a tirade about how "women these days" are ruining everything.

The unspoken rules of the Fragility Olympics are as absurd as they are exhausting. First, overreact to everything. If someone says they don't like your favorite movie, don't just shrug it off, declare it a personal attack on your taste and intelligence. If someone suggests you could benefit from being a bit more open-minded, take it as a direct challenge to your authority and retaliate accordingly. Second, double down on bad opinions. If you've been called out for saying something offensive or misinformed, never admit you were wrong. Instead, dig in your heels, raise your voice, and insist that you're being persecuted for "telling it like it is." And finally, when all else fails, punch something. It could be a wall, a table, or even the air, what matters is that you've demonstrated your raw, unbridled masculinity in a way that impresses absolutely no one.

At the heart of this competition is an endless need for validation, wrapped in the guise of confidence. But let's be honest: this isn't confidence, it's insecurity wearing a cheap alpha mask. Real confidence doesn't require constant posturing or a running tally of imagined victories over trivialities. It doesn't demand that you assert dominance in every conversation or prove your toughness with performative outbursts. What you're displaying isn't strength; it's fragility, plain and simple. And the louder you shout, the more obvious it becomes.

The Fragility Olympics thrive on this paradox: the men most determined to appear unshakable are the ones most easily rattled. You've built your identity around a definition of manhood so narrow it can't withstand the slightest pressure. A pink drink, a rainbow flag, or a woman speaking her mind becomes a threat not because these things are inherently offensive, but because your sense of self is so precariously constructed. It's as if you've built your masculinity out of glass and then set up a target range around it. Every perceived challenge shatters a little more of the illusion, and instead of repairing it, you just yell louder, insisting that everyone else is the problem.

What's truly ironic is how much effort you put into convincing the world, and yourself, that you're unbothered. You wear your "alpha" persona like a suit of armor, but it's made of papier-mâché, and everyone can see it falling apart. Your manhood isn't threatened by pink drinks or sunscreen; it's threatened by your own refusal to embrace vulnerability, growth, and nuance. You've trapped yourself in a caricature of masculinity, one where strength is measured by how loudly you can shout "facts don't care about your feelings" before storming out of the room. But here's a fun fact: real strength doesn't require shouting, and it definitely doesn't require storming out. It requires staying in the room, listening, and sometimes, even when it's uncomfortable, admitting that you're wrong.

The tragedy of the Fragility Olympics is that it doesn't have to be this way. You could choose a different path, one where masculinity isn't defined by how easily you're provoked or how loudly you defend your bad opinions. You could let go of the need to prove yourself at every turn and focus instead on building a sense of self that isn't so easily shaken. But that would require effort, introspection, and a willingness to challenge the very ideas that brought you here. And let's face it, that's not the kind of heavy lifting you're interested in.

As we move forward, consider this: What would happen if you stopped competing? If you stepped out of the Fragility Olympics and decided to redefine manhood on your own terms? What if you embraced strength not as a performance, but as a quiet, steady confidence rooted in authenticity and self-awareness? The answer might surprise you. Or it might terrify you. Either way, it's worth exploring, because the alternative is to keep playing a game no one respects, for a prize no one wants. Stay tuned.

The Tools of Fragility

The tools of fragility are as predictable as they are exhausting, and you wield them with the precision of someone who's spent years mastering the art of avoidance. Let's start with your go-to weapon: bad opinions on repeat. You cling to your arguments like a drowning man clings to a log, even when those arguments are sinking under the weight of facts. When someone challenges you with evidence, your reflex is to snap back with "Facts don't care about your feelings," all while ignoring the actual facts. The irony would be hilarious if it weren't so sad. You're not defending your position because it's right; you're defending it because admitting you're wrong feels like admitting defeat, and in your world, that's the ultimate threat to your masculinity.

But your greatest hits don't stop there. Let's talk about anger, the mask you wear to cover your insecurities. For you, anger isn't just an emotion; it's a performance. You slam doors, punch walls, and raise your voice not to resolve anything but to assert dominance. What you don't realize is that none of this makes you look strong, it makes you look scared. Anger is the easiest emotion to access because it requires no introspection. It's a convenient shortcut to avoid facing the uncomfortable truths about yourself. But here's the thing: real strength isn't about how loudly you can yell or how hard you can hit. It's about staying composed and in control, especially when things don't go your way. Of course, calm doesn't earn you applause in the Fragility Olympics, does it?

Your insecurities extend far beyond anger. They seep into your need to control others, especially women. Nothing terrifies you more than a woman who's smarter than you, more educated, or, heaven forbid, independent. If she's assertive, you call her aggressive. If she earns more than you, it's a threat. If she rejects you, she's "damaged" or "too picky." And if she dares to have a degree or career that overshadows yours? Suddenly, she's "too educated." You twist her success into an insult, as if her achievements exist solely to diminish you. But it's not her ambition that's the problem, it's your fragile ego. Instead of seeing a smart, capable woman as a potential partner or equal, you see her as a challenge to your identity. Your need to control and diminish others is a desperate attempt to avoid confronting how little control you have over yourself.

And of course, the stage for all this fragility is social media, the ultimate arena for your performance. Your online presence isn't about connecting with others or sharing meaningful insights; it's about posturing. Every post, every comment, every tweet is carefully curated to reinforce your worldview and draw applause from your echo chamber. You measure your worth in likes, shares, and comments, treating social media as both a battlefield and a scoreboard. But no matter how many followers you gain or arguments you "win," it's never enough. Social media doesn't satisfy your insecurities, it amplifies them. You're stuck in a cycle of seeking validation, receiving it, and immediately needing more. Instead of building relationships or learning something new, you're just competing, endlessly, in a game that offers no real rewards.

The saddest part of all this is how ineffective these tools of fragility are. You think they make you look strong, but they don't. They make you predictable, shallow, and stuck in a loop of your own creation. Your bad opinions, your anger, your need to control others, and your obsession with online validation aren't signs of toughness, they're signs of avoidance. You're avoiding growth, vulnerability, and the uncomfortable but necessary work of redefining what it means to be a man. Every tantrum, every rant, every refusal to engage in meaningful dialogue only reinforces the insecurities you're trying to hide. And the funniest part? You're the only one who doesn't see it. Everyone else is watching, shaking their heads, and, yes, laughing, because nothing is more absurd than someone claiming strength while wielding the tools of fragility like a sword made of glass.

You're not winning the Fragility Olympics, by the way. There are no winners in this competition. The more you lean into these behaviors, the more you lose: relationships, opportunities, and the chance to become a better version of yourself. What you call strength is nothing more than a carefully constructed façade, one that cracks under the slightest pressure. Instead of fixing the cracks, you just add more layers of bravado, hoping no one will notice. But here's the truth: we've noticed. Everyone has. And the more you rely on these tools, the more obvious it becomes that you're not the strong, confident man you pretend to be. You're fragile, scared, and clinging to an identity that isn't serving you.

It doesn't have to be this way. You could put down these tools and pick up something more meaningful: introspection, empathy, and the courage to face yourself as you truly are. It's not easy, and it won't happen overnight, but it's worth it. Because the tools of fragility won't make you stronger, they'll only keep you trapped in the same cycle of insecurity and avoidance. So, what's it going to be? Are you going to keep competing in the Fragility Olympics or finally start building something real? The choice is yours.

Winning the Fragility Olympics

Congratulations, you've done it, you've mastered the art of avoiding accountability and are well on your way to claiming the gold medal in the Fragility Olympics. The rules are simple, and you follow them flawlessly. First, never apologize. Admitting fault would mean acknowledging imperfection, and your fragile sense of self can't handle that kind of honesty. If someone points out your mistakes, deflect. If someone calls you out, double down. The blame is never yours, it's society, feminism, cancel culture, or that woman who dared to reject you. In your world, accountability is for "betas," and you're far too busy maintaining the illusion of dominance to bother with self-reflection. It's a perfect system for staying stuck because it allows you to sidestep any meaningful growth while continuing to blame the world for all your problems.

Your strategy works, at least on the surface. By refusing to admit fault, you've constructed a persona that seems impervious to criticism. You present yourself as the alpha male, the guy who never makes mistakes and never backs down. But let's be honest: that's not strength. That's fear disguised as confidence. Real strength comes from owning your actions, acknowledging your flaws, and striving to do better. What you call dominance is really just insecurity wearing a mask, and it's not fooling anyone. The people around you can see through it. They know that your refusal to apologize isn't a sign of power, it's a desperate attempt to protect your fragile ego. And the more you cling to this strategy, the more obvious your insecurities become.

This brings us to the great paradox of your fragile masculinity: the harder you work to project strength, the more transparent your vulnerabilities are. When you shout over others in a debate, it doesn't make you look powerful; it makes you look scared of being wrong. When you refuse to take responsibility for your actions, it doesn't make you seem untouchable; it makes you seem immature. When you turn every disagreement into a contest to prove your dominance, you're not demonstrating confidence, you're showing just how deeply your sense of self is tied to external validation. The louder you yell, the more people see through the cracks in your façade. Real strength doesn't announce itself; it doesn't need to. It speaks quietly through actions, humility, and resilience. But humility doesn't get you applause in the Fragility Olympics, does it?

Your tactics don't just highlight your insecurities, they amplify them. Every time you refuse to take accountability, you're reinforcing the very behaviors that keep you stuck in this endless cycle of fragility. It's like building a house of cards and then acting shocked when it collapses. Your obsession with avoiding blame, asserting dominance, and maintaining the illusion of strength doesn't make you stronger, it makes you brittle. The smallest challenge, the slightest critique, and the whole structure starts to wobble. But instead of addressing the foundation, you just stack more cards, hoping no one will notice how fragile it all is.

The consequences of this mindset go far beyond your personal identity. Fragile masculinity isn't just your problem; it's everyone's. It poisons relationships, creating cycles of toxicity where accountability and communication should thrive. How can you build a healthy partnership when you're too busy deflecting blame or turning every disagreement into a battle for control? How can you foster trust when you're unwilling to show vulnerability or admit when you're wrong? You can't. Your refusal to take responsibility doesn't just hurt you, it hurts the people around you, too. Partners, friends, family, they all feel the impact of your unwillingness to grow. Relationships built on a foundation of deflection and dominance are doomed to fail because they lack the honesty and mutual respect needed to thrive.

But the ripple effects don't stop there. This mindset also stalls societal progress. A culture rooted in fragile masculinity can't adapt to change, embrace diversity, or foster innovation. When masculinity is reduced to a performance, a checklist of outdated ideals and shallow displays of dominance, it leaves no room for growth. It rejects inclusivity, dismisses compassion, and resists anything that challenges the status quo. This isn't strength; it's stagnation. And it's holding everyone back. A society that values appearances over substance, control over collaboration, and rigidity over resilience is one that will inevitably crumble under the weight of its own contradictions. Your obsession with maintaining this performance of manhood isn't just unsustainable, it's detrimental to everyone around you.

What makes it even sadder is how much energy you pour into maintaining this charade. You spend countless hours rehearsing your performance, perfecting your comebacks, and posturing for an audience that isn't even paying attention. Every social media post, every debate, every attempt to assert your dominance is part of a relentless cycle that leaves you exhausted and unfulfilled. And yet, you keep going, convinced that if you just try a little harder, yell a little louder, or post a little more, you'll finally achieve the validation you crave. But you won't.

The applause will never be enough because the real problem isn't external, it's internal. You're not battling society, feminism, or cancel culture. You're battling yourself, and until you address that, nothing will change.

Here's the truth: this performance of manhood is hollow. It doesn't fulfill you, it doesn't serve you, and it doesn't make you happy. It's a never-ending race to nowhere, fueled by insecurities you refuse to confront. And the saddest part? You don't even realize how much it's costing you. You're sacrificing real connections, personal growth, and the chance to become a better version of yourself, all for the sake of maintaining an illusion that no one respects. Your fragile masculinity isn't a shield; it's a cage, and you're the one holding the key. The question is, will you use it? Or will you keep competing in a game that has no winners, only losers who are too afraid to face the truth?

Your obsession with dominance extends beyond the Fragility Olympics, shaping your ideals, relationships, and view of the world. Spoiler: it's just as hollow as your alpha aspirations. But there's hope, if you're willing to let go of the performance and start building something real. The question is, are you ready to step off the podium and start doing the work? Because if not, the only thing you'll be left holding is that fragile trophy, and trust us, it's not worth it.

Myths About Masculinity You Need to Unlearn
"Real men don't cry." – Emotions are human, not gendered. Suppressing them doesn't make you stronger.
"Strength means never showing weakness." – True strength comes from acknowledging and addressing your vulnerabilities.
"Being dominant means being respected." – Respect is earned through empathy, integrity, and collaboration, not intimidation.
"Men are the providers, women are the nurturers." – Gender roles are outdated; partnerships thrive on shared responsibilities.
"Masculinity is about physical strength." – It's about resilience, emotional intelligence, and adaptability, not just muscle mass.
"Apologizing is a sign of weakness." – Taking accountability shows maturity and strength, not fragility.
"Men should always be in control." – Life is unpredictable, and trying to control everything leads to frustration, not fulfillment.
"Asking for help is unmanly." – Seeking help shows courage and a commitment to growth.
"Men should never back down." – Knowing when to compromise or walk away is smarter than needless conflict.
"Only betas care about self-care." – Taking care of yourself isn't optional; it's essential for mental and physical health.
"Men should always have the answers." – No one knows everything. Being open to learning is far more valuable than pretending.
"Masculinity is about being stoic." – Expressing emotions fosters deeper connections and understanding.
"Men shouldn't be stay-at-home parents." – Parenting is a shared role, and being present is a strength, not a sacrifice.
"Men must always win." – Life isn't a competition; collaboration often leads to greater success.
"Real men drink beer and eat steak." – Preferences don't define masculinity; enjoy what makes you happy.
"Pink is for girls." – Colors are colors, not gender statements. Wear pink, eat yogurt, and relax.
"A man's worth is measured by his paycheck." – Your value is in your character, not your income.
"Men shouldn't show affection to other men." – Friendship, love, and support aren't limited by gender.

"Men are naturally better leaders." – Leadership is a skill, not a birthright, and it thrives on humility and cooperation.
"If you're not an alpha, you're a failure." – The alpha/beta dichotomy is a myth. Be authentic, not performative.
"Men should always be the initiators." – Relationships thrive on mutual effort; it's not solely on men to take the first step.
"Men shouldn't show emotion in public." – Vulnerability isn't a private act; it's a human one, and it belongs everywhere.
"Real men never lose." – Losing gracefully builds character and resilience; no one wins all the time.
"Men can't multitask." – This stereotype limits your potential. Men are perfectly capable of handling complex tasks simultaneously.
"Men are naturally more logical than emotional." – Logic and emotion coexist in everyone, and valuing both leads to better decisions.
"Men don't need to communicate their feelings." – Clear communication builds stronger relationships and prevents unnecessary conflict.
"It's unmanly to enjoy 'feminine' hobbies." – Cooking, dancing, or reading aren't unmanly, they make you interesting.
"Men are always ready for sex." – Sexuality is complex and personal. Pressure to conform to this myth can harm mental and emotional health.
"Men who fail aren't trying hard enough." – Failure is part of growth, and it's not a reflection of your worth or effort.
"Real men never compromise." – Compromise shows wisdom, maturity, and respect for others, not weakness.

Feel Free to Draw A Picture of Yourself Winning Below

Feel Free to Draw a Picture of Your Manhood Below

Chapter 7
The Brocial Justice Warrior Fighting for Men's Rights

The Men Too Movement – A Manifesto of Misunderstanding
The "Men Too" movement is your rallying cry for justice, or at least your version of it, which is more about grievances echoing unchecked than any actual pursuit of fairness. Welcome to the parody of legitimate social justice, where your motto, "Equality, but for us!" declares a bold new era of rights for those already holding most of the cards but feeling personally victimized when someone else gets a seat at the table. If your movement had a flag, it would probably be a gym towel hastily scrawled with "Stop the Matriarchy!" And your mascot? A guy in a "Saturdays Are for the Boys" T-shirt yelling indignantly at a rainbow flag. This is the Men Too movement, something nobody asked for but no one can escape because you just won't stop shouting.

Your slogans are where it gets particularly absurd. "Stop the matriarchy!" you cry, as if women secretly run the world from their Pinterest boards and book clubs. "Men are the real victims!" you declare, even while sitting comfortably atop most societal hierarchies. The sheer ridiculousness of these rallying cries is matched only by the decibel level at which you deliver them. What's conspicuously absent, of course, is any substance. There's no data, no coherent argument, just yelling. But in your world, volume equals validity. If you shout loud enough, surely it must be true. Or at least, that's what you're betting on.

But let's cut to the heart of it: what are you really fighting for? That's the question you never seem to answer. When asked about your endgame, you launch into a vague tirade about "false accusations," "biased family courts," or "the feminization of society." Press for details or evidence, though, and the conversation collapses into a mess of buzzwords and grievances that don't add up. What you actually want, it seems, is a space where you can air your frustrations without anyone challenging you. Accountability? Out of the question. Solutions? Not your department. What you're clinging to is a form of victimhood that's exaggerated and performative, turning every minor inconvenience into an existential crisis. In your world, a woman getting a promotion is a direct assault on men, and a romantic rejection is clear proof of systemic oppression.

The foundation of your movement is its most fragile feature. It's built on a deep misunderstanding of equality, where giving others the same opportunities you've always enjoyed feels like a personal loss. You see progress for marginalized groups not as a step forward for society but as a threat to your dominance. Equality, in your mind, is a zero-sum game, if someone else gains, you must be losing. But equality isn't a pie; giving others a slice doesn't mean you have less. It means everyone gets a piece. Try explaining that, though, and you'll retreat to your favorite rebuttal: "It's not fair!" Because to you, fairness means maintaining the status quo where you're always at the top.

And here's the irony: you borrow so much from the movements you claim to oppose. You've adopted the language of activism, complete with slogans, hashtags, and rallies, but you've stripped it of any real meaning. Your grievances feel real to you, but they lack the systemic context or historical weight of genuine social justice issues. Instead, you inflate personal disappointments into societal crises and frame yourself as a martyr in a battle that doesn't actually exist. You're not fighting for justice, you're fighting for attention, for validation, and for the right to rage without being questioned.

Let's talk about your favorite boogeyman: "the matriarchy." According to you, it's the shadowy force responsible for everything from your professional setbacks to your romantic failures. Never mind that there's no evidence of its existence. The idea that women secretly wield all the power is laughable, especially when you look at actual statistics about inequality. But facts don't matter in your echo chamber. What matters is the feeling of being wronged, even if that feeling stems from nothing more than insecurity and entitlement. If you can blame the matriarchy, you don't have to look in the mirror.

And then there's your fixation on false accusations, your favorite trump card whenever your arguments start to fall apart. You portray a world where men live in constant fear, one wrong move away from having their lives destroyed by vindictive women. Never mind that false accusations are statistically rare; in your narrative, they're an epidemic. It's a fearmongering tactic designed to stoke resentment, conveniently ignoring the fact that the vast majority of harassment and assault survivors are women who face disbelief and victim-blaming. But nuance isn't your strong suit. You'd rather weaponize fear than confront the uncomfortable realities of systemic inequality.

At its core, the Men Too movement isn't about fighting for rights. It's about resisting accountability. It's a backlash against progress, a reflexive response to a world that's moving toward equality. You don't want to share power, opportunities, or space, you want to hoard them under the guise of protecting yourself. But here's the thing: this mindset doesn't just hurt others; it hurts you, too. By clinging to outdated notions of dominance and masculinity, you're trapping yourself in a cycle of anger, resentment, and isolation. You're not just fighting against progress; you're fighting against your own potential for growth.

And as you grow louder, your movement becomes harder to take seriously. The slogans, the outrage, the performative victimhood, they're all distractions from the real issues facing society. Instead of creating a movement that addresses genuine challenges, you've built a parody of activism, one that prioritizes ego over empathy and noise over nuance. It's a movement fueled by misunderstanding, but the biggest misunderstanding of all is your own: the idea that equality is something to fear.

How to Host Your Own Men Too Rally

If you're planning to host your own Men Too rally, you'll need a roadmap to navigate the chaos of baseless grievances and performative theatrics. Don't worry, there's a well-worn playbook for turning hollow outrage into the illusion of legitimacy. Follow these steps, and you'll be the talk of the manosphere, at least until someone else yells louder than you. Let's break it down.

Step 1: Ignore the Facts

Facts are your greatest enemy, so leave them at the door. When organizing a Men Too rally, the first rule is to avoid evidence at all costs. Statistics, historical context, and peer-reviewed studies are dangerous, why let pesky reality interfere with your narrative? Instead, stick to anecdotal evidence and unverified claims. Someone, somewhere once said something that validates your grievance? Perfect, build your entire argument around it. If someone challenges you with actual data, deflect by making it personal. Say things like, "Why can't men share their truth without being silenced?" or, "Your statistics don't reflect what's happening to real men." The key is persistence. Repeat your point louder and more passionately, no matter how thoroughly it's been debunked. Remember, in the Men Too playbook, feelings trump facts every time.

Step 2: Loud Equals Right

In the world of Men Too, volume is your strongest weapon. Why debate when you can drown out your opponents by shouting? The louder you speak, the more legitimate your argument appears, at least to your fellow rally attendees. When faced with dissent, rhetorical deflections are your best friends. "What about men?" is a classic, implying that addressing one issue invalidates all others. Another favorite is cherry-picking anecdotes: find a single example of a man facing hardship, and use it as proof that society is biased against your entire gender. Context is irrelevant; what matters is creating the appearance of a systemic issue. And when someone calls out your flawed logic, accuse them of being biased, part of the "feminist agenda," or simply incapable of understanding your struggle. It's not about winning the argument, it's about exhausting the opposition.

Step 3: Performative Outrage
If volume is your sword, outrage is your shield. Nothing says "legitimate movement" like a dramatic display of indignation. Whether it's a monologue about how men are the real victims of society or a public stunt that makes zero practical sense, the goal is to grab attention. Bonus points if your outrage involves props, like protest signs with slogans such as "Stop the Matriarchy!" or "Equality, but for us!" Theatrics matter here. The more over-the-top your performance, the more likely you are to attract an audience. Sure, they might be watching out of morbid curiosity, but attention is attention, right? Just make sure you don't have to back up your outrage with action, this is about noise, not solutions.

Step 4: Declare Victory Prematurely
The Men Too movement thrives on hollow victories. As soon as your opponent grows tired of your shouting, declare success. If they walk away, claim it's because they couldn't handle your "truth." If they block you on social media, tell your followers it's proof they were "silencing men." Exhaustion is your endgame, and disengagement is your trophy. The point isn't to win hearts and minds; it's to outlast everyone else. Declare victory loudly and often, even when it's obvious to everyone else that you've achieved nothing. After all, in the echo chamber of the Men Too movement, perception is reality.

In the end, hosting a Men Too rally isn't about advocating for real change or addressing genuine grievances, it's about creating a spectacle. The louder, angrier, and more persistent you are, the more successful your rally will seem, at least to those already on your side. And if you're lucky, you might even convince yourself that your shouting, deflections, and outrage add up to something meaningful. But here's the reality: the Men Too rally is less about rights and more about the performance of victimhood. Congratulations, you've mastered the art of making noise without making a difference.

The Brocial Justice Warrior Playbook

The Brocial Justice Warrior playbook is your ultimate guide to transforming baseless outrage into an identity, victimhood into a strategy, and privilege into a complaint. It's not about fighting for real justice or creating meaningful change; it's about ensuring your grievances take center stage while avoiding accountability at all costs. Let's break down the tactics you rely on to keep the illusion alive.

First and foremost, you excel at weaponizing anecdotes. When confronted with the reality that your claims don't hold up to scrutiny, you reach for a single, dramatic story, whether it's relevant or not, and use it as a stand-in for a larger, nonexistent crisis. Can't find real data to support your argument? No problem. Someone, somewhere, had an experience that sort of aligns with what you're saying, and that's enough to declare an epidemic. Facts might derail your narrative, so you avoid them at all costs. Instead, you lean into emotional appeals and personal stories that are impossible to verify or disprove. When someone challenges your logic, your immediate response is to make it personal: "Why are you trying to silence men like me?" You don't need evidence when you can shift the focus to your feelings. After all, if you feel oppressed, it must be true.

Another favorite strategy is reframing privilege as persecution. Whenever someone asks you to share power or space, you interpret it as a personal attack. Progress for others feels like oppression for you because, in your mind, equality is a zero-sum game. If someone else is gaining, you must be losing. That's why you shout about "the matriarchy" even though it doesn't exist, and why you see every advancement for women or marginalized groups as a direct threat. It's easier to claim you're being persecuted than to admit you've always benefited from the system. You're not fighting to change anything; you're fighting to keep things exactly as they are, under the guise of protecting your rights.

Of course, none of this would be possible without the echo chambers you rely on. You surround yourself with like-minded voices that amplify your grievances, validate your outrage, and insulate you from criticism. Whether it's an online forum, a social media group, or a podcast, these spaces give you the constant reassurance that your feelings are justified and your worldview is correct. You don't engage with opposing perspectives because it's easier to stay in a bubble where no one challenges you. Instead, you and your fellow warriors build a self-sustaining cycle of outrage. Someone posts an anecdote that confirms your biases, you share it with a dramatic caption, and the comments roll in with unanimous agreement. It's a feedback loop, where every grievance becomes amplified and every doubt is silenced.

This echo chamber doesn't just protect your beliefs, it magnifies them. By spending so much time in these spaces, you convince yourself that your struggles are more widespread and urgent than they actually are. You see yourself as a warrior in a fight that no one else understands, a defender of men's rights in a world gone mad. But outside your bubble, your arguments fall apart. The slogans that seem so powerful in your forum sound ridiculous in the real world, and the outrage you thrive on comes across as petty and performative. You think you're leading a movement, but in reality, you're just shouting into the void with people who already agree with you.

Here's the harsh truth: your movement is hollow. For all the noise you make, you're not actually accomplishing anything. You don't have policies to propose, solutions to offer, or even a clear vision for what you want to achieve. Your energy goes into venting rather than building, complaining rather than creating. Imagine what you could accomplish if you directed that energy toward real issues, advocating for mental health resources for men, challenging toxic masculinity, or pushing for workplace policies that benefit fathers. Instead, you waste it on performative victimhood, chasing a sense of justice that never materializes because it's rooted in grievance, not action.

The hollowness of your fight is most evident in the way it damages your credibility. By framing yourself as a perpetual victim and refusing to engage constructively, you alienate potential allies and undermine your own cause. Even the issues you claim to care about, like men's mental health, get overshadowed by your constant need to play the victim. You turn what could be meaningful advocacy into a parody of itself, reducing men's rights to a joke. Instead of addressing real challenges, you spend your time yelling about imagined threats and blaming others for your unhappiness. It's not a movement; it's a tantrum.

And here's the kicker: all of this, the outrage, the echo chambers, the performative victimhood, isn't just damaging your credibility. It's damaging your relationships, your growth, and your ability to engage meaningfully with the world around you. By clinging to this hollow fight, you're isolating yourself from real solutions and real connections. And yet, your insecurities don't stop here. They spill over into how you see the world, how you interact with others, and how you shape your vision for society. What happens when your need for dominance and victimhood extends beyond personal grievances? Stay tuned, because we're about to explore how this mindset shapes not just your movement but the culture you're trying to control.

Feel Free to Draw a Picture of Yourself as a Victim Below

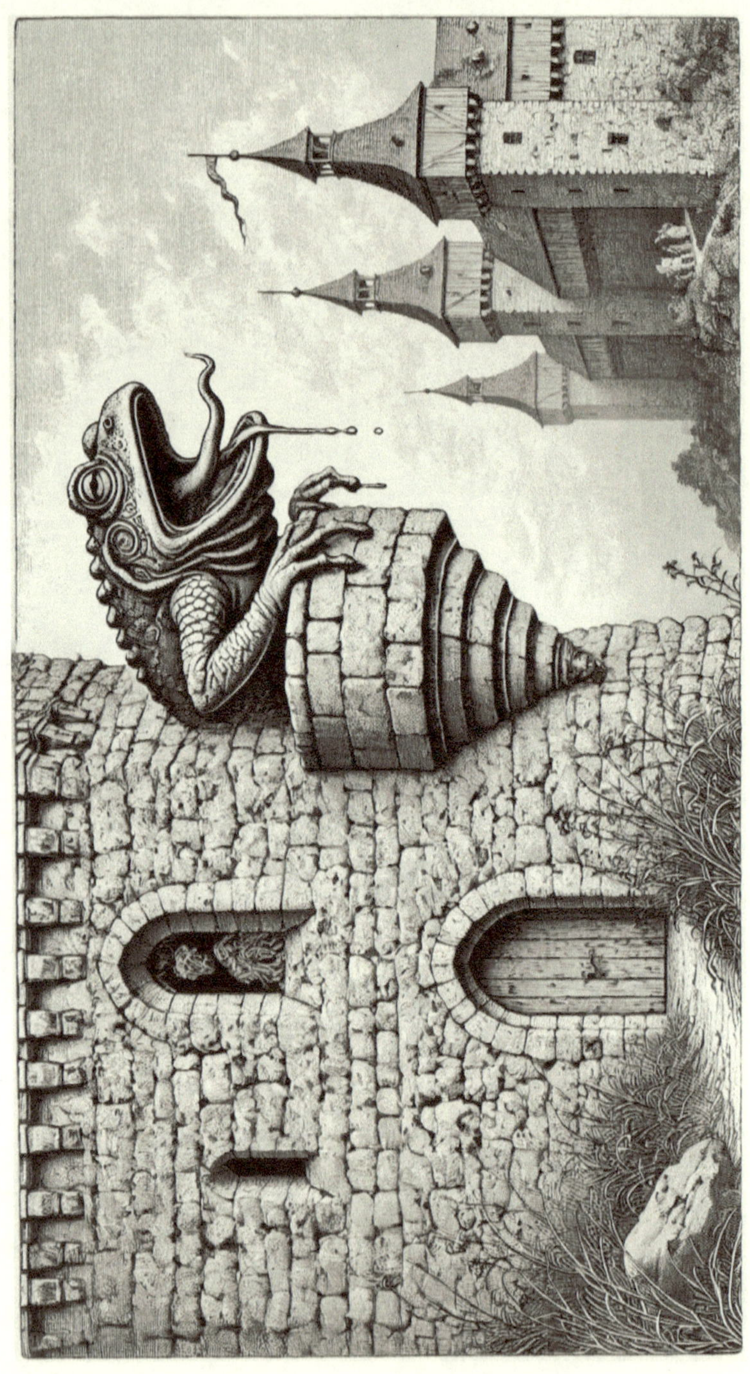

Chapter 8
Mansplaining Your Way to Success But But But DEI

The Art of Mansplaining

Mansplaining isn't just a habit for you, it's your battle cry, your bread and butter, your go-to strategy for making sure every room you walk into knows you're *there.* And if someone calls you out for it? You've got your excuse locked and loaded: blame DEI. Diversity, Equity, and Inclusion becomes your catch-all scapegoat for everything that's ever gone wrong in your life. Didn't get that promotion? Clearly, the company's DEI policy is at fault. Someone dared to correct you? That's just the DEI agenda making it impossible for men like you to succeed. Forget accountability; you've got acronyms to blame.

At its core, mansplaining is your way of maintaining control in a world you feel is slipping away from you. DEI is the convenient villain you've chosen to rail against, the bogeyman responsible for all your perceived injustices. It doesn't matter that DEI initiatives are about fostering inclusion and dismantling barriers. To you, they're just a threat, an excuse to explain why the world isn't bending to your will. And in your quest to stay relevant, you use mansplaining as your weapon of choice, dominating conversations and silencing dissent, all while grumbling about how unfair it is that you even have to share space with people who don't look, think, or act like you.

Classic mansplaining scenarios take on a whole new flair when DEI enters the mix. You're not just interrupting a woman to explain her own idea, you're "fighting back" against the supposed tyranny of inclusivity. Correcting someone with lived experience? That's just you pushing back against the "softness" DEI has introduced into professional spaces. In your mind, every interruption, every condescending explanation is a necessary stand against what you see as an unfair advantage given to anyone who isn't exactly like you. Never mind that you're wrong nine times out of ten; it's not about being right. It's about being *heard*, even if it means stomping on everyone else's voice to do it.

And why does mansplaining "work" for you? Because it creates the illusion of authority in a world where you feel increasingly irrelevant. It's not about adding value to conversations or demonstrating expertise, it's about making sure your voice drowns out the ones you've convinced yourself don't belong. DEI becomes your punching bag, a way to externalize blame and avoid any introspection. When people disengage from your interruptions, you interpret their exhaustion as victory, never stopping to ask whether your tactics are pushing people away rather than drawing them in.

But your reliance on DEI as a scapegoat doesn't stop at the workplace. It leaks into every corner of your life, turning social interactions into battlegrounds where you can't resist declaring how DEI is ruining everything. At a party, you explain why inclusivity is "dumbing down" standards, even as you can't remember the last time you actually read a book on the topic. On social media, you post tirades about how men like you are being "canceled" for speaking the truth, oblivious to the fact that what you're really being called out for is your inability to share the stage. Your worldview becomes a closed loop of grievance, where every critique of your behavior is reframed as an attack on your masculinity and every disagreement is proof that DEI is out to get you.

The irony, of course, is how much energy you pour into fighting a concept you barely understand. DEI isn't responsible for your failures, your own refusal to adapt and grow is. But instead of confronting that uncomfortable reality, you double down, using mansplaining as both a shield and a sword. You weaponize your interruptions to assert dominance and deflect criticism, mistaking loudness for leadership and condescension for competence. DEI isn't the enemy here, it's your refusal to see past your own insecurities and recognize that the world isn't rigged against you. You're not losing because of inclusivity; you're losing because you refuse to compete on a level playing field.

And here's the real kicker: for all your complaints about DEI, it's not DEI policies that are holding you back, it's your own arrogance. Mansplaining doesn't make you look strong or knowledgeable; it makes you look desperate. Your insistence on blaming DEI for every setback reveals more about your insecurities than it does about the state of the world. You're not standing up for yourself, you're avoiding the hard work of self-reflection and growth. Every time you interrupt, every time you condescend, every time you blame DEI for your shortcomings, you're reinforcing the very barriers you claim to fight against.

So go ahead, keep mansplaining your way through life. Blame DEI for everything from your stalled career to the fact that people walk away mid-conversation. Convince yourself that the problem isn't you but a world that's somehow unfairly tilted against men like you. You're so profoundly clueless about this topic, you probably can't even spell DEI, let alone know what it stands for or truly understand it. And when the opportunities dry up, when the relationships crumble, when the rooms grow quieter and the echo chambers grow louder, you can sit back and blame DEI one more time. But deep down, you'll know the truth: it was never DEI. It was always you.

Building a Lifestyle Around Mansplaining

Mansplaining isn't just your go-to move, it's your entire strategy for navigating life, work, and social interactions. In the professional world, you've turned it into an art form, confidently claiming credit for ideas that aren't yours and explaining concepts to people who clearly know more than you. Why? Because you've convinced yourself that it's not expertise that matters, it's being the loudest voice in the room. And when your behavior finally gets called out, you've got a ready-made excuse: blame it on DEI. After all, how could you be expected to thrive in a workplace that dares to prioritize collaboration, equity, and respect over your relentless need to dominate every conversation? Surely, the system must be rigged.

But let's not give DEI all the credit (or blame) for your behavior, mansplaining thrives on a much broader stage. It starts with your deeply ingrained belief that confidence is a substitute for competence. You've internalized the mantra that acting like you know what you're talking about is more important than actually knowing it. Got nothing useful to contribute in a meeting? No problem, just speak louder, sprinkle in some buzzwords, and watch as people reluctantly nod along. It doesn't matter if your points are redundant, irrelevant, or flat-out wrong. What matters is that you're speaking, and in your mind, speaking equals leading. And when someone dares to correct you or push back? That's when you trot out the old "DEI agenda is stifling free speech" line, deflecting attention from your own lack of substance.

Mansplaining isn't just a professional tool for you, it's a lifestyle. At family gatherings, you'll happily explain how to carve a turkey to the relative who's hosted Thanksgiving for decades. On first dates, you'll launch into a monologue about cryptocurrency or your gym routine, completely missing the fact that your date has checked out five minutes in. At work, every team meeting is another opportunity to restate someone else's point as though you've just had a groundbreaking epiphany. It's not about contributing meaningfully, it's about making sure your voice is heard, no matter how unwelcome or unnecessary it is. Every interaction becomes a stage for your performance, and you play the same tired role every time: the self-proclaimed expert who doesn't realize how little he knows.

But while you're busy perfecting your craft, the people around you are paying the price. Every time you interrupt someone to mansplain, you're silencing their voice. Every time you take credit for an idea, you're undermining the contributions of others. And every time you monopolize a conversation, you're draining the energy of everyone forced to endure your monologue. Women, in particular, bear the brunt of this behavior, navigating a world where their expertise is constantly questioned and their perspectives are routinely dismissed. And let's not forget the colleagues who roll their eyes and exchange knowing glances whenever you start explaining something obvious. They're tired, not just of you, but of the culture that allows you to thrive unchecked.

Even worse, you've convinced yourself that you're the victim here. If a woman walks out of the room mid-mansplanation, you don't think, "Maybe I should rethink my approach." No, you blame DEI for creating an environment where your genius is underappreciated. If a team doesn't respond enthusiastically to your hijacking of a project, it's not because you've alienated them, it's because the system is unfair to men like you. You turn every critique of your behavior into proof that you're being silenced, when in reality, people are just exhausted from listening to you.

The irony, of course, is that your insistence on mansplaining isn't just hurting others, it's hurting you. The more you talk over people, the more you alienate them. The more you dismiss other perspectives, the less you learn. And the more you rely on mansplaining as a substitute for real expertise, the more obvious your insecurities become. You're not building respect or authority, you're eroding it, one condescending comment at a time. Sure, you might get away with it for a while, but eventually, people will stop engaging with you altogether. They'll smile politely, nod occasionally, and then move on with their lives, leaving you to stew in your echo chamber of self-congratulatory nonsense.

And here's the kicker: DEI isn't your enemy. It's not the reason people roll their eyes when you talk or why your colleagues disengage when you interrupt. That's all you. DEI isn't silencing you, it's giving others the space to speak, and your ego can't handle the competition. The truth is, you're not being edged out by inclusivity; you're being edged out by your own refusal to adapt. You've mistaken dominance for leadership and loudness for authority, and it's left you stuck in a cycle of performative expertise that benefits no one, not even you.

So go ahead, keep mansplaining your way through life. Keep blaming DEI for every setback, every awkward silence, and every person who stops returning your calls. But deep down, you know the truth. It's not the system that's holding you back, it's your own inability to listen, learn, and grow. The world isn't against you. It's just tired of putting up with your nonsense. And if you keep this up, the only person left in your audience will be yourself. But hey, at least you'll have someone to mansplain to.

The Limits of Mansplaining

Mansplaining might feel like your ticket to dominance, but let's take a moment to reflect on what happens when the performance collapses. Because, spoiler: it does. Imagine confidently explaining a concept to someone only to have them point out, in front of everyone, that they wrote the book on it, literally. Or think about that meeting where you hijacked the discussion, only to be met with stony silence and a palpable wave of resentment. These moments of mansplaining backfire aren't just awkward, they're career kryptonite. Instead of gaining authority, you're left scrambling to rebuild credibility, often with the very people you dismissed. Worse yet, every time you double down with excuses, like blaming DEI for "shifting the rules," you dig yourself into a deeper hole. No one's buying it. They see through the bravado, and what they see isn't impressive, it's embarrassing.

The real problem with mansplaining is that it traps you in a cycle of arrogance and failure. You interrupt, overexplain, and dominate conversations because you think it's how leaders act. But every time you bulldoze over someone else's input, you're not building bridges, you're burning them. Collaboration? That's off the table. Growth? Forget it. You're too busy clinging to the illusion of control to actually learn from those around you. Instead of fostering respect, you foster resentment. Your colleagues avoid you, your friends stop sharing with you, and anyone with the misfortune of being in your personal or professional orbit quickly learns to tune you out. You think you're projecting strength, but what you're actually showing is a desperate need for validation at the expense of meaningful relationships.

And let's not pretend this behavior exists in a vacuum. Mansplaining doesn't just harm you; it harms the spaces you occupy. Workplaces where your antics thrive are often rife with frustration, inefficiency, and disengagement. Imagine a team where every idea has to survive your interruptions or where progress slows to a crawl because someone has to pause and endure your 20-minute monologue on a subject you barely understand. DEI initiatives, which aim to level the playing field and amplify marginalized voices, only make this tension more obvious. When you shout down or dismiss others, you're not just ignoring DEI principles, you're undermining the very collaboration and respect that drive success. And every time you blame DEI for your declining influence, you confirm what everyone already suspects: your problem isn't inclusivity. It's you.

The cost of mansplaining extends beyond the workplace. It seeps into personal relationships, eroding trust and connection. Whether it's a partner, a friend, or a family member, people eventually get tired of being talked at instead of listened to. The more you insist on dominating every conversation, the more isolated you become. Relationships require reciprocity, and mansplaining leaves no room for it. You're not engaging, you're performing. And when people stop clapping, all you're left with is the echo of your own voice. The loneliness this creates isn't a side effect, it's the inevitable consequence of prioritizing dominance over understanding.

So let's address the hollow victory you've been chasing. Sure, in the moment, mansplaining might feel like you've won something. You've held the floor, asserted your "expertise," and maybe even silenced someone who dared to challenge you. But what did you actually gain? A fleeting sense of superiority? A brief moment where you felt in control? Meanwhile, your relationships deteriorate, your credibility crumbles, and the respect you so desperately crave becomes increasingly out of reach. This is the paradox of mansplaining: it feels like power but functions as weakness. It isolates you, limits you, and leaves you ineffective in the very spaces where you're trying to thrive.

Here's the question you need to ask yourself: If mansplaining is your measure of success, what does failure look like? Because from the outside, the distinction isn't clear. The louder you talk, the less people listen. The more you interrupt, the more you're ignored. The more you blame DEI or external factors for your struggles, the more obvious it becomes that you're missing the point entirely. Success isn't about being the loudest or the most dominant, it's about being the most effective, and you can't achieve that when your tactics actively alienate everyone around you.

So maybe it's time to step back and reconsider your approach. Because while mansplaining might get you through the occasional meeting or awkward conversation, it's not a foundation you can build anything meaningful on. It's a crutch, a defense mechanism, and ultimately, a hollow performance that leaves you with nothing but the sound of your own voice echoing back at you. Maybe that's enough for you. But if it's not, then it's time to stop talking and start listening.

Feel Free to Draw a Picture of Yourself Talking Normal Below

Chapter 9
The Ultimate Chad's Guide to Reproductive Rights

Control Without Accountability

Reproductive rights are gone, and somehow, you're still complaining. It's almost remarkable, the mental gymnastics required to celebrate the stripping of women's autonomy while simultaneously whining about the consequences of your own behavior. Did you imagine that a world where women are forced to carry pregnancies caused by rape, incest, or abuse would somehow leave you unaffected? Did you think that by cheering for laws that prioritize control over compassion, you'd be exempt from the moral and social fallout? Here's a hard truth for you: those who deny freedom to others don't escape the consequences of that denial themselves. While women are enduring systemic cruelty under these new laws, you're still out here grumbling, as if the real victim in all of this is you.

Let's address the grim realities you conveniently ignore. Over 90% of sexual assaults are perpetrated by men. One in four women in the United States has experienced sexual violence, and one in three has endured physical violence by an intimate partner. When it comes to incest, child abuse, and trafficking, the statistics remain damning: men overwhelmingly make up the majority of perpetrators. And yet, you still have the audacity to act like this is a "man vs. woman" issue, spinning narratives about false accusations and "unfair" child support laws while refusing to confront the epidemic of violence perpetrated by your own gender. Instead of acknowledging the horrors of rape survivors forced to carry pregnancies or young girls enduring childbirth after incest, you focus on your grievances, deflecting blame and responsibility at every turn. How do you rationalize celebrating these atrocities while demanding to be seen as the victim?

Your favorite pastime is the blame game. When unplanned pregnancies occur, you act like you weren't involved. When a woman demands child support, you paint yourself as oppressed by a system rigged against men. Paternity tests? Those must be part of some feminist conspiracy, right? You've mastered the art of dodging accountability, convincing yourself that every consequence of your actions is someone else's fault. But let's be clear: you demand control over women's reproductive choices while refusing to accept any responsibility for your own role in reproduction. It's not just hypocrisy; it's cruelty. By denying the link between your behavior and the outcomes you complain about, you perpetuate a cycle of harm that leaves women, and society as a whole, to clean up your mess.

Your stance on birth control is just as contradictory. You expect women to shoulder the full burden of preventing pregnancy, from invasive procedures to managing the side effects of hormonal contraception. But condoms? Too inconvenient. Vasectomies? Too emasculating. Meanwhile, you cheer for laws that strip women of access to contraception and abortion, creating a world where their choices are erased, and their lives are dictated by your negligence. And let's not forget the devastating toll this takes on survivors of violence. Pregnancies resulting from rape or trafficking are treated with the same disregard as consensual ones, forcing victims to endure unimaginable trauma. But you, with your loud demands for control and silent complicity in cruelty, still manage to cast yourself as the aggrieved party. If accountability were a test, you'd fail before you even opened the book.

And then there's your obsession with control. Let's not pretend that your support for these laws is about morality or justice, it's about dominance. You didn't want equality or fairness; you wanted power. You wanted to dictate the terms of reproduction while escaping the consequences. But control without accountability is nothing more than tyranny. The new reality you've championed isn't just cruel, it's barbaric. Women are being forced to carry pregnancies caused by rape. Children are being denied agency over their own bodies. Survivors of abuse are being retraumatized by a legal system that prioritizes ideology over humanity. And yet, you sit back and complain about how unfair life is for you. It's a level of entitlement so grotesque it would be laughable if it weren't so harmful.

Your deflection tactics extend to every corner of your life. When confronted with the systemic violence perpetrated by men, you shout about false accusations or cry "not all men" as if that absolves you of the collective responsibility to address these issues. You demand freedom for yourself while celebrating the removal of freedom for women, mothers, daughters, and sisters. You preach about the importance of personal responsibility while refusing to take any. You cheer for laws that force rape survivors to give birth, then complain about how the "system" oppresses men. Your rhetoric is hollow, your actions are cruel, and your hypocrisy is glaring.

And let's talk about the broader consequences of your behavior. By enabling or outright supporting these laws, you're not just harming women, you're undermining trust in relationships, families, and communities. The world you've helped create is one where fear and resentment thrive, where the most vulnerable are left unprotected, and where your obsession with control leaves everyone worse off, including yourself. You've traded compassion for cruelty, fairness for dominance, and responsibility for deflection. And what do you have to show for it? A reputation as someone who talks loudly about freedom but does everything in their power to deny it to others.

Here's the brutal truth: your refusal to take accountability doesn't make you strong, it makes you weak. It doesn't make you dominant, it makes you dangerous. And it doesn't make you a victim, it makes you complicit. Women are enduring atrocities under the laws you champion, from forced pregnancies to the silencing of their voices in the face of violence. Meanwhile, you continue to whine about fairness, oblivious to the suffering you've helped inflict. You claim to stand for freedom, but the only freedom you truly care about is your own.

So here you are, railing against a system that occasionally holds you accountable while cheering for a system that strips women of their rights. The irony is staggering, but the harm is even greater. Your refusal to grow up, to take responsibility, and to confront the consequences of your actions has left a trail of pain and injustice that no amount of excuses can erase. Reproductive rights may be gone, but the consequences of your choices remain. The question isn't whether you'll ever take responsibility, the question is whether you'll ever understand the damage you've done. Spoiler: it's unlikely. But don't worry, when you're finally left to face the reality you've created, there will be no shortage of people to remind you where it all went wrong. Good luck explaining this one to the daughters, sisters, and wives whose lives you've helped devastate.

Self-Help for the Reproductively Irresponsible

Congratulations, you've reached the self-help section for navigating the dystopian nightmare you helped create. Reproductive rights have been stripped away, women are enduring barbaric new laws that violate their autonomy, and you're still somehow finding a way to complain. If you've ever thought, "Why should I deal with the consequences of my actions when I can blame women, society, or a grand feminist conspiracy?" then this satirical guide is for you. Step one: deny everything. No matter how obvious the evidence, dig in your heels and declare it fake. DNA tests? Rigged. Court orders? Misinterpreted. The law itself? Clearly biased against men. Step two: disappear. Can't deny it anymore? Just ghost the situation. Leave the mother of your child to deal with the chaos you helped create, while you vanish into a smug cloud of self-pity and delusion. Step three: scream about how "the system is rigged" at anyone who'll listen, as if that absolves you of the basic responsibilities of adulthood.

Your playbook is a masterpiece of hypocrisy. You cheer for the cruel removal of women's reproductive rights, celebrating their loss of autonomy as some kind of victory for your worldview. You call it justice or morality, but what it really is, is barbarism dressed up as righteousness. You revel in the power to control women's choices while screaming about your own "freedom" being under siege. Freedom, for you, is a one-way street. You demand it for yourself while actively or complicitly denying it to the women you claim to love, your wives, sisters, daughters, and mothers. The contradictions are so glaring it's almost impressive how completely you manage to ignore them.

Let's talk accountability, or your lack of it. You've built an entire identity around the idea that responsibility is for "betas." Admitting fault? That's weakness. Taking care of the consequences of your own choices? Not your style. You cling to the myth that real men never apologize or own up to their actions, all while demanding absolute control over women's lives. It's a twisted paradox: you want the power to dictate the rules, but you refuse to abide by them yourself. And when the inevitable consequences of your irresponsibility come knocking, you deflect, deny, and disappear, leaving others to clean up your mess.

Your financial irresponsibility is just as hypocritical as your moral posturing. You celebrate policies that strip women of their rights and force them into impossible situations, all while doing everything in your power to avoid paying child support. You rail against the system as though it's oppressing you, but the reality is far simpler: you just don't want to spend money on anything that doesn't directly benefit you. You'll spend hours scheming to dodge your financial obligations, filing frivolous claims, and concocting conspiracy theories about biased courts, all to avoid doing the bare minimum. Meanwhile, the women you've abandoned are left to carry the financial and emotional weight of raising children alone. Your actions don't just hurt them; they hurt the very children you claim to care about. But sure, keep telling yourself you're the victim.

And let's not forget the rhetorical gymnastics you perform to justify your behavior. You cast yourself as a misunderstood martyr, a lone wolf fighting against a system that's out to get you. You cry about how unfair life is while cheering for laws that make women's lives unbearable. You accuse women of weaponizing the legal system, even as you weaponize it yourself to avoid accountability. Your entire narrative is built on lies, half-truths, and a refusal to confront your own shortcomings. You're not a hero; you're a caricature, clinging to outdated ideals that crumble under the weight of reality.

What's most shocking, and yet somehow entirely predictable, is how little you seem to care about the barbaric conditions women are enduring because of the laws you support. You celebrate these draconian measures as "restoring order" or "protecting life," but you ignore the human cost. The mothers, wives, daughters, and sisters you claim to respect are being denied life-saving healthcare, forced to carry pregnancies against their will, and subjected to government control over their bodies, and you applaud it. Meanwhile, you can't even handle the responsibility of paying child support or showing up for your own kids. The hypocrisy is staggering, but the lack of self-awareness is even worse.

Your tactics might give you short-term wins, avoiding financial consequences, dodging accountability, and keeping your ego intact, but the long-term costs are devastating. Your refusal to take responsibility damages relationships, alienates your children, and leaves a trail of broken trust that no amount of rhetorical posturing can repair. The women in your life see through you, even if you think they don't. Your children will grow up with questions you'll never have good answers for. And society as a whole will continue to pay the price for the chaos you helped create, all because you were too afraid to face the consequences of your actions.

So here you are, clutching your hollow victories and shouting into the void about how unfair it all is. The system you claim is rigged against you isn't perfect, but it's not the problem, you are. Your refusal to take responsibility, your celebration of cruelty, and your relentless hypocrisy have left you isolated, bitter, and powerless. But don't worry, you've got your echo chamber to fall back on, where your grievances will always find an audience. Just don't expect anyone outside it to take you seriously.

Because at the end of the day, the joke is on you. While you're busy dodging accountability and celebrating the loss of women's rights, the world is moving forward without you. And when the consequences of your actions finally catch up, as they always do, you'll have no one to blame but yourself. Good luck explaining that to your kids, or to the mirror.

The True Cost of Dodging Responsibility

The true cost of dodging responsibility stretches far beyond your personal failures. It seeps into your relationships, corrodes society, and lays bare the cruel hypocrisy of your worldview. Your refusal to take accountability doesn't just harm the people closest to you; it undermines the very concept of freedom you claim to champion. You scream about liberty, individual rights, and government overreach, yet you celebrate, or remain complicitly silent, while women, mothers, wives, daughters, and sisters are stripped of their fundamental freedoms. You demand your rights but turn a blind eye when those rights are denied to others. Your double standard isn't just glaring; it's an affront to the very ideals of justice and equality you pretend to uphold.

Let's unpack this hypocrisy. You rail against any infringement on your autonomy, yet you champion laws that dictate what women can and cannot do with their bodies. You claim to despise government interference, yet you support, or fail to oppose, the most invasive forms of control over women's lives. You cry out against oppression when it suits you but ignore the daily oppression faced by half the population. The freedom you claim to cherish is nothing more than a selfish illusion, where liberty applies only to you and not to anyone else.

This isn't just about reproductive rights; it's about your entire approach to accountability. True responsibility means standing up, not just for yourself, but for others. It means being a role model for other men, demonstrating what it looks like to own your actions and stand for what's right. It means calling out other men for their atrocious behavior, even when it's uncomfortable or inconvenient. When you laugh at their misogyny, share their toxic rhetoric, or reward their cruelty with likes, clicks, and votes, you're not just endorsing their behavior, you're empowering it. You're giving them a platform to spread their harm further, to erode justice more deeply, to poison society more completely.

Being an ally to women isn't optional if you care about equality and freedom. It means listening, supporting, and taking action to dismantle the systems that oppress them. It means challenging the narratives that perpetuate misogyny and refusing to stand by while women are dehumanized. It means rejecting the "boys will be boys" mentality that excuses terrible behavior and stepping up to hold yourself, and others, accountable. This isn't about being a hero; it's about being decent. It's about doing the bare minimum to create a world where everyone, not just you, can thrive.

Your refusal to act doesn't just harm women, it weakens the very fabric of society. When you celebrate the loss of women's autonomy, you undermine families, communities, and progress itself. The wives, mothers, daughters, and sisters you claim to love are left navigating a world where their choices are stolen, their futures are constrained, and their humanity is ignored. And what about you? You might think this doesn't affect you, but it does. A society that denies freedom to one group will eventually deny it to others. Your silence, your inaction, and your complicity don't just hurt women; they set the stage for broader injustices that will inevitably circle back to you.

Responsibility isn't a burden, it's an opportunity to lead, to build, to inspire. When you step up and demand better, you show other men what it looks like to be strong in the ways that matter. When you reject the voices of cruelty, misogyny, and injustice, you weaken their grip on power. When you refuse to amplify their hate, you rob them of the influence they crave. And when you stand with women, you demonstrate the kind of courage and integrity that can change the world. That's the real test of character: not how loudly you can shout about your own freedom, but how fiercely you can fight for the freedom of others.

The truth is, your silence speaks volumes. It tells the world that you're okay with oppression as long as it doesn't affect you. It tells women that their struggles are invisible to you, their voices unimportant. It tells other men that it's fine to look the other way when injustice happens. But here's the reality: silence is complicity. Every time you fail to act, you're choosing the side of the oppressor. Every time you prioritize your comfort over someone else's freedom, you're endorsing the status quo. And every time you refuse to hold other men accountable, you're enabling the very behavior that keeps society stuck in cycles of harm.

What do you gain from this complicity? A fleeting sense of power? The satisfaction of avoiding discomfort? Deep down, you know it's all hollow. The freedoms you cling to will one day come under threat, and there will be no one left to stand with you. The women you ignored, the men you let off the hook, the systems you upheld, they could have been your allies. But by then, it will be too late. You'll find yourself isolated, surrounded only by the echoes of your excuses and the weight of your inaction.

Freedom isn't a zero-sum game. It doesn't shrink when it's shared; it grows. Responsibility isn't a punishment; it's the price of integrity. Until you understand this, you're not just failing yourself, you're failing everyone who looks to you for leadership, for allyship, for hope. The question isn't whether you'll take responsibility; it's whether you'll take it before it's too late. Because if you don't, the only legacy you'll leave behind is one of complicity, hypocrisy, and failure.

Responsibility means recognizing that your actions, or inactions, ripple far beyond your immediate circle. When you dismiss accountability, you're not just letting down those who depend on you; you're signaling that doing the bare minimum is acceptable. Younger men, colleagues, peers, they look to you as an example, whether you realize it or not. Choosing apathy, self-interest, or silence in the face of injustice gives others permission to do the same. But when you model courage, integrity, and allyship, you inspire others to rise. Imagine a world where men stand up for what's right, call out what's wrong, and refuse to tolerate harmful behavior. You have the power to set that standard and show that decency and accountability aren't optional, they're essential. Standing up for women and girls, being a decent guy, and choosing respect over ridicule? That's sexy, attractive, and simply the right thing to do.

Being a role model isn't about grand gestures or public statements. It's about private choices that define who you are when no one's watching. It's calling out misogyny in conversations, even if it makes others uncomfortable. It's refusing to laugh at sexist jokes, even if everyone else does. It's rejecting systems and policies that strip women of their rights, even when inconvenient. Rewarding cruelty and oppression fuels harm. Real strength isn't ignoring injustice, it's confronting it until change becomes inevitable.

Feel Free to Draw a Picture of Yourself Being Nice Below

Chapter 10
Bro Culture
The Manosphere's Echo Chamber

Bro Flix: The Cinema of the Manosphere

Bro Flix is your Hollywood, the cinematic shrine to everything you hold dear: alpha males saving the day, explosions drowning out introspection, and a world where complexity and nuance are just pesky details to be ignored. This is your safe haven, where masculinity reigns supreme, women are either conniving villains or subservient prizes, and every storyline assures you that your worldview is not only valid but heroic. It's a formula designed to soothe, to affirm, and to protect you from the discomfort of reality. In the world of Bro Flix, there are no shades of gray, no complex moral dilemmas, no challenges to your belief system, just loud, flashy affirmations of a world that caters to your every insecurity.

The formula for Bro Flix is as predictable as it is comforting. You've got your male savior, usually a rugged, brooding figure who embodies strength, dominance, and a disdain for modernity. He's the guy who steps in when the world has gone soft, corrupted by progress, overrun by "woke" agendas, and teetering on the edge of collapse. His mission? To reclaim what's been lost, to reassert order, and to remind everyone what real power looks like. The action is explosive, the dialogue is sparse and gruff, and the storylines are recycled from the same tired tropes you've been fed for decades. Superhero reboots are your bread and butter, offering the illusion of reinvention while delivering the same old narratives of male heroism and female expendability. Conspiracy thrillers are another favorite, where lone alpha males take on shadowy organizations that threaten their freedom, their family, or their fragile sense of control. And let's not forget the nostalgia-fueled sequels that drag beloved franchises back from the dead, ensuring you never have to confront anything new or challenging.

At the heart of Bro Flix lies a recurring antagonist: the villainous woman. She's always there, lurking in the shadows, plotting the downfall of the male hero or undermining his mission with her intellect, ambition, or independence. Whether she's a conniving professional with a Ph.D., a cold and calculating boss, or a seductive femme fatale, her role is always the same: to serve as a threat to masculinity. She's not a person; she's a symbol, a stand-in for everything you fear about the modern world. Her intelligence is emasculating, her power is threatening, and her autonomy is intolerable. She exists not as a fully realized character but as a one-dimensional barrier for the male hero to overcome. The message is clear: women who step out of their traditional roles are dangerous, and the only way to restore balance is for the man to triumph over them. It's a tired, predictable trope, but one that reassures you by reducing complex human beings into easily defeatable obstacles.

Bro Flix thrives on simplicity, offering you an escape from the complexities of real life. These movies don't ask you to think, to question, or to grow, they ask only that you sit back and let them validate your beliefs. The world they present is one where strength is always physical, solutions are always violent, and emotions are always a liability. There's no room for introspection, no acknowledgment of the gray areas that define real human experiences. Instead, you get a fantasy of dominance, a world where men are always in control, always right, and always justified. It's a comforting illusion, but one that keeps you trapped in a cycle of shallow gratification and unexamined assumptions. By refusing to engage with complexity, Bro Flix reinforces your resistance to change and growth, ensuring that you remain exactly where you are, unchallenged, unfulfilled, and unwilling to confront the deeper truths about yourself and the world around you.

And yet, as soothing as Bro Flix may be, it's just one piece of a much larger puzzle. The same ideas that shape these movies, about dominance, simplicity, and the villainization of women, are echoed across the broader cultural landscape of the manosphere. From podcasts to social media influencers, the themes of Bro Flix spill over into every corner of the ecosystem that caters to your insecurities and feeds your fantasies. It's not just the movies you watch; it's the podcasts you listen to, the influencers you follow, and the content you share. Bro Flix is the starting point, the gateway drug to a culture that celebrates your grievances and shields you from growth. So, enjoy the explosions and the alpha heroes, but remember: the world outside your cinematic bubble is far more complicated, and far more rewarding, than the one these movies portray. If you're willing to step outside the echo chamber, you might just find that real strength lies not in dominating others but in understanding them.

Bro Flix Classics

Hollywood's commitment to serving up Bro Flix masterpieces is nothing short of relentless. It's as if the entire industry decided to abandon nuance and complexity in favor of delivering tailor-made narratives that stroke your ego while fueling your grievances. If you're looking for titles that reinforce your worldview, keep your insecurities intact, and ensure that you never have to confront your own flaws, Bro Flix has you covered.

First up is *Cancel Culture Island: The Movie*, a cinematic spectacle where self-proclaimed alphas are stranded on a remote island crawling with their worst nightmare: feminists armed with accountability and razor-sharp retorts. The plot unfolds as the men, convinced of their "rightful" dominance, attempt to outwit their challengers while fumbling through pointed questions like, "Why does equality scare you so much?" Their grand plans for island supremacy unravel in hilariously spectacular fashion, as yelling louder and flexing harder prove ineffective against logic and self-awareness. The tagline? "Survival of the Fragile." Spoiler alert: accountability wins every time.

In *Alpha Males Gone Wild: The Movie,* self-proclaimed alphas gather for the ultimate showdown of absurd dominance, competing in challenges like chest-thumping marathons and heated latte debates over what's "manly." The events escalate into primal scream-offs, grueling push-up wars, and laughably staged feats of "alpha grit." As the battles intensify, their desperation to outdo each other transforms into a comedic spectacle of egos imploding under their own weight. The grand finale crowns the "winner," a lone man standing in a puddle of insecurity, who triumphantly receives a cracked mirror trophy, symbolizing his refusal to face reality. It's peak Bro Flix: hilariously overblown and wildly entertaining.

No Bro Flix lineup would be complete without a deep dive into the endless ocean of superhero reboots. These movies cater to your longing for simplicity, a world where the good guys punch the bad guys, and moral complexity is solved with a well-timed explosion. Superheroes offer you a fantasy of effortless dominance, where power is inherent, and responsibility is optional. It's the ultimate escape from real-world problems, wrapped in CGI and spandex. The dialogue might be predictable, and the plots recycled, but none of that matters because the hero is always a guy who gets the girl, saves the day, and never has to question his place in the universe. It's comfort food for the soul, served up in IMAX.

And then there are the dystopian conspiracy thrillers, a Bro Flix staple designed to scratch your paranoia itch. These films always follow the same formula: the system is rigged, men are the victims, and only a lone alpha male can expose the truth. Never mind that the "system" in these stories is often so poorly defined that it's more of a vague vibe than an actual conspiracy. What matters is that it gives you someone to blame for everything that's wrong in your life. Whether it's shadowy government forces, an evil corporation run by, you guessed it, a powerful woman, or a vague allusion to "woke culture," these movies let you revel in the fantasy of righteous rebellion without ever asking you to consider whether you might be part of the problem. It's cathartic, sure, but it's also pure escapism masquerading as insight.

These titles are more than just entertainment, they're mirrors held up to the manosphere's values and fears. They're designed to reassure you that your grievances are valid, your worldview is correct, and your place at the center of the story is deserved. But here's the kicker: while you're busy immersing yourself in these cinematic comfort zones, the world keeps moving forward. Real progress is happening off-screen, and the longer you stay glued to these narratives, the further behind you fall. You can keep watching, of course. Hollywood will gladly keep feeding you these stories as long as you demand them. But maybe it's time to change the channel, or at least ask yourself why you're so invested in these fantasies to begin with.

Bro Podcasts: Amplifying the Echo

Bro podcasts have become the ultimate megaphone for the manosphere, a tool to amplify grievances, cement toxic ideologies, and ensnare listeners in an echo chamber of self-reinforcing nonsense. Podcasts are unique in their intimacy; they offer long-form, seemingly unfiltered discussions that give the illusion of authenticity and personal connection. This format makes them one of the most effective ways for the manosphere to peddle its worldview. They position themselves as platforms for "truth," "free speech," and "debate," yet the reality is far from it. These podcasts are carefully curated echo chambers, not arenas for open discussion, and they operate more like propaganda arms than independent voices.

The rise of the bro podcast was no accident. As traditional media began to demand accountability and nuance, the manosphere seized the opportunity to carve out a space where its rhetoric could thrive unchecked. Popular examples like *The*

Joe Rogan Experience, *Fresh & Fit*, and Andrew Tate's various shows epitomize this shift. Joe Rogan bills himself as a curious everyman, hosting lengthy conversations that oscillate between genuine curiosity and conspiracy-mongering. Rogan's platform often amplifies fringe ideas and pseudo-science, creating a space where listeners can feel "informed" without critically engaging with the content. Then there's *Fresh & Fit*, which markets itself as a dating and lifestyle guide but serves primarily as a megaphone for bitterness and overt misogyny. Andrew Tate's offerings, meanwhile, take toxic masculinity to an extreme, celebrating dominance, hustle culture, and an explicit disdain for women. Tate's carefully curated image as a hyper-masculine influencer has been further tainted by his recent legal detainment and charges related to human trafficking, rape, and organized crime. These allegations expose the disturbing reality behind his rhetoric, underscoring the harm perpetuated by figures who glorify control and exploitation. What unites these podcasts is their ability to package toxic messages with just enough humor, charisma, and pseudo-intellectualism to make them not only palatable but compelling to their audiences, allowing dangerous ideas to flourish under the guise of "free speech" and entertainment.

What makes bro podcasts particularly insidious is their reliance on the cult of personality. Hosts don't just present themselves as commentators; they become idols, leaders, and even pseudo-fathers to their audiences. This is not by accident. These figures are experts at wielding charisma to draw in listeners and create a sense of camaraderie. They appear unpolished enough to seem relatable but are calculated in their rhetoric to ensure they remain the dominant voice in their audience's lives. Humor is often their gateway, disarming the listener and making them feel like they're sitting down with a buddy. But beneath the laughs lies a darker purpose: to validate grievances, reinforce toxic beliefs, and position themselves as the only reliable source of truth in a world they claim is out to silence men. By presenting themselves as "unfiltered" and "real," they sidestep accountability for their harmful messages, painting criticism as an attack on free speech rather than a legitimate response to their actions.

One of the most dangerous aspects of bro podcasts is their fusion of misinformation and entertainment. They mix half-truths with humor, creating a potent cocktail that's difficult for listeners to parse critically. Whether it's cherry-picking data to fit their narratives, citing dubious studies, or sharing outright fabrications, these hosts excel at making the absurd sound plausible. They thrive on anecdotes over evidence, spinning personal experiences into sweeping generalizations that listeners accept as universal truths. This combination of casual delivery and serious claims makes it easy for audiences to absorb harmful ideas without realizing they're being manipulated. It's a bait-and-switch tactic: come for the laughs and camaraderie, stay for the conspiracy theories and manufactured outrage. And once you're in, it's hard to leave. The humor and parasocial connection create a sense of loyalty that makes listeners resistant to opposing viewpoints.

This loyalty is what makes bro podcasts so effective at building parasocial relationships. Listeners don't just hear the hosts; they feel like they know them. The format of podcasting, with its long, unbroken conversations, creates an illusion of intimacy. It's like being part of a private chat among friends, except only one side is talking. This dynamic fosters a deep sense of trust, making listeners more likely to internalize the hosts' beliefs and less likely to question them. Criticism of the host becomes personal, as listeners see it as an attack on someone they "know" and admire. This emotional investment creates a feedback loop where the audience becomes more entrenched in the manosphere's worldview, rejecting alternative perspectives as threats to their newfound identity.

And let's dispel the myth that these podcasts are independent voices fighting against "woke" censorship or mainstream control. The reality is that many of the most prominent bro podcasts are bankrolled by wealthy conservative interests with a vested agenda. These aren't grassroots operations; they're corporate-backed projects designed to shape public opinion, particularly among disenfranchised men who feel left behind by modern society. These podcasts play into the manosphere's anti-establishment rhetoric while being anything but independent. Their hosts rail against the "mainstream" while cashing checks from donors and advertisers with deep pockets and darker motives. This dynamic makes the entire enterprise not just hypocritical but deeply manipulative. The very men who pride themselves on their anti-sheep mentality are being herded into ideological pens by those who see them as nothing more than useful tools in a larger political game.

This manufactured rebellion extends to the topics these podcasts obsess over. Whether it's railing against feminism, complaining about cancel culture, or fantasizing about a return to traditional gender roles, the content is carefully curated to keep listeners angry and engaged. But this focus on grievance over growth comes at a cost. Listeners are encouraged to see themselves as perpetual victims, locked in a battle against a society that doesn't appreciate them. This narrative is both comforting and disempowering. It gives men an easy scapegoat for their problems while robbing them of the tools they need to address those problems meaningfully. Instead of fostering resilience, these podcasts cultivate resentment. Instead of encouraging self-improvement, they validate stagnation. The result is a cultural bubble that grows thicker and more impenetrable with each episode.

The ultimate irony is that bro podcasts, which pride themselves on promoting freedom, individuality, and critical thinking, do the exact opposite. They don't challenge their listeners; they coddle them. They don't encourage diverse perspectives; they shut them out. And they don't foster independence; they create dependence, on the hosts, on the ideology, and on the carefully curated narrative that keeps the manosphere thriving. It's a deeply cynical enterprise, and its success comes at the expense of its audience's growth, happiness, and understanding of the world.

So here you are, tuned in, laughing along, nodding in agreement, and feeling like you've found your tribe. But at what cost? The laughs fade. The camaraderie is one-sided. And the sense of purpose you think you've found is hollow, built on a foundation of half-truths and someone else's agenda. The question isn't whether these podcasts are entertaining, they are. The question is whether the entertainment is worth the price of your own critical thinking and the integrity of your worldview. Because as long as you're listening, the echo chamber will keep growing louder, drowning out the voices that might actually challenge you to be better.

Bro Social Media Influencers: The Feed of Toxicity

The rise of bro social media influencers isn't accidental; it's a calculated marketing machine for the manosphere, designed to normalize and celebrate toxic masculinity. Through viral videos, motivational posts, and grindset culture, these influencers deliver their messages to millions. Platforms like TikTok, YouTube, and Instagram amplify their content, making it entertaining, engaging, and dangerously persuasive. Whether it's a quick clip on "dominating" relationships or a rant against feminism, these influencers have mastered the art of packaging harmful ideas into digestible content that feels personal and compelling.

TikTok's algorithm thrives on virality, turning short clips into widespread toxicity. Influencers dole out "alpha tutorials" peppered with pseudo-psychology to sound credible, leaving little room for critical thinking. YouTube offers longer formats for deep dives into anti-feminist rants and grindset sermons, while Instagram serves as a showroom for gym selfies, luxury goods, and an unattainable version of masculinity. Together, these platforms create a trifecta of influence, reinforcing a narrow definition of manhood rooted in dominance, wealth, and physical perfection. Every post is crafted to lure you into a world where the surface matters more than substance and where aspiration is just another word for manipulation.

These platforms don't just host content, they actively amplify it. Algorithms prioritize engagement, meaning divisive, extreme posts rise to the top. Viral soundbites and trends distill complex issues into inflammatory memes, turning stereotypes into shareable moments. The result is a digital ecosystem where misogyny and performative masculinity thrive, unchecked and incentivized. Bro influencers focus on aesthetics over substance, using lavish lifestyles and gym gains to project an image of control that's as intimidating as it is hollow. The endless displays of luxury and physical perfection aren't about aspiration, they're about intimidation, making you feel like you're failing if you don't match their curated success. The more unattainable the image, the more dependent you become on their guidance.

At the heart of this ecosystem is the economics of attention. Bro influencers aren't just selling ideas; they're monetizing themselves. Clicks and views fuel ad revenue and sponsorships, creating a perverse incentive for increasingly extreme content. Controversy becomes currency, authenticity is sacrificed for virality, and the influencers you follow become entrepreneurs selling insecurities back to you. Far from being independent thinkers, many are backed by wealthy interests, religious conservatives and corporate elites with agendas to manipulate public policy. The so-called "free thinkers" railing against "the system" are, in truth, cogs in a machine exploiting your vulnerabilities. Their rebellion isn't against oppression but against introspection, creating a cycle where you're distracted from questioning anything meaningful.

This commodified masculinity shapes culture, particularly among young men. Bro influencers become role models for boys and teenagers, teaching them to equate self-worth with dominance and material success. This aspirational standard leaves no space for vulnerability or empathy, creating insecurities that fuel the manosphere's growth. These messages harm not just women but also men, locking them into cycles of frustration and toxic behavior, all while promising a success that's both unattainable and meaningless. The influence is pervasive, embedding itself into how you view relationships, measure success, and define your identity. The false promises lead you further from authentic fulfillment and closer to a curated caricature of masculinity.

Perhaps the most insidious aspect of bro influencer culture is its ability to create echo chambers. Algorithms ensure that once you engage with this content, you're flooded with more, isolating you from opposing perspectives. This bubble validates and magnifies your grievances, turning minor frustrations into hardened ideologies. Influencers become your tribe, their opinions gospel, and their approval your goal. These parasocial relationships make you resistant to criticism, convinced that challengers are enemies. It's not just manipulation; it's isolation, engineered to keep you dependent on a system that thrives on your doubts and insecurities.

The facade of authenticity in bro influencer culture is damaging. Their lives are curated to appear relatable, using calculated storytelling and selective vulnerability to draw you in. They present themselves as self-made heroes who've overcome adversity, conveniently ignoring the privilege or corporate backing behind their success. This crafted relatability blurs the line between entertainment and manipulation, making you believe their path is accessible if you hustle hard enough, even as it sets unattainable standards. Your admiration feeds their empire while leaving you feeling inadequate for falling short of their curated fantasy. Beyond personal harm, this toxicity corrodes society, normalizing misogyny, glorifying dominance, and rejecting empathy, fostering division and oppression for fleeting validation. Their version of masculinity isn't liberating; it's a cage, trapping you in insecurities that fuel their profits.

Coming Soon: 'Culture' You Might Like:

Movies

Alpha's Endgame

In a dystopia ruled by women, one bro rallies gamers to "restore order." Gym montages, evil female scientists, and a steak ban ensue. Spoiler: He cries over lost protein powder.

The Matrix: Bro Reloaded

A "reimagining" where the red pill turns men into alphas battling an AI that cancels door-holders. Scenes include rants against sunscreen, pink drinks, and feelings.

Crypto Gladiators

Bros fight in a coliseum of debt to reclaim their crypto millions. Cameos feature influencers pitching NFTs mid-battle.

Beta Bloodlines

A horror flick where "weak men" are hunted by a force called Accountability. Twist: The monster is their reflection.

Freedom Siege

One alpha defends his town from "woke mobs" teaching gender studies. Signature line: "Over my dead, gym-toned body."

Podcasts

Grindcast: Wake, Lift, Repeat

Two bros ramble about hustle culture and their failed crypto empires. Guests include steroid peddlers and "finance gurus" pushing pyramid schemes.

Feminist Apocalypse Radio

A 90-minute meltdown blaming women's autonomy for society's collapse. Weekly dictator admiration segment included for "strong leader vibes."

The Cancelled Chronicles

Bros complain about cancel culture while earning millions. Features disgraced influencers whining about accountability.

Bro Philosophy 101

Misquotes Nietzsche to justify ghosting women and gym obsession. Recent hits: "Socrates Was a Sigma" and "Plato on Protein."

Alpha Airwaves
Hosts scream at callers for being "beta." Tips: "Eat elk liver, drop emotions, and dominate everything."

Influencers
@CryptoChad420
Shirtless, screaming in front of rented Lamborghinis. Claims to be a self-made millionaire but forgets to mention his trust fund. Posts gems like: "Women only want MONEY, MUSCLE, and SILENCE."
@TheRedPillSavior
Charges $500 for "alpha courses" plagiarized from old self-help books. Tagline: "Don't be her Plan B, be her Plan F (for Fearless)."
@LiftOrLeave
Posts gym videos with captions like, "If she hates your gains, drop her." Famous for bad form and worse advice but somehow millions of fans.
@FreedomFratboy
Rants against "big government" in five-second TikToks. Burns books he can't pronounce while draped in an American flag.
@CancellordSupreme
Debunks feminist "lies" (aka facts) and sells overpriced "Alpha Fuel" protein powder that's mostly sugar.

Manosphere Books: Titles No One Asked For
Gains Over Brains – Skip thinking, lift heavier.
Crypto and Chill – Lose money, blame society.
The Alpha Almanac – Wake at 4 AM; ignore feelings.
Cancel Culture Survival Guide – Crying without looking weak.
Dating for Dummies – Be so "alpha" you're undatable
Grindset Gospel – Sleep is for losers; burnout is for alphas.
How to Gaslight and Win – Denial tactics for the fragile male ego.
Red Pill Recipes – Steak, protein powder, and tears.
Alpha Leadership for Betas – Shout louder, think less.
Flex First, Apologize Never – A guide to making enemies everywhere.

Chapter 11
Brotopia
Building Your Own Man Cave Nation

Welcome to Brotopia

Brotopia, the manosphere's ultimate fantasy, has come to life. This is a land where men reign unchallenged, free from the "constraints" of equality and the presence of women. On paper, it's a utopia of endless freedom, male solidarity, and the absolute rule of alpha dominance. In reality, it's a disaster of epic proportions, a chaotic experiment in unchecked egos and short-sighted decision-making. Without women to blame, assist, or stabilize the society, Brotopia has become a crumbling monument to the pitfalls of toxic masculinity. The dream of this "perfect" male-only world quickly unravels into a dystopian landscape defined by dysfunction, infighting, and a baffling inability to maintain even the most basic forms of civilization.

The vision for Brotopia was ambitious in its simplicity: a world where men could thrive without interference. The founding principles, however, reveal its inherent contradictions. Brotopia's constitution proclaims, "All men are created equal, except betas, simps, and anyone who admits to having emotions." It's a land where dominance is celebrated, vulnerability is punished, and the mere suggestion of compromise is met with suspicion. Crying is banned, collaboration is mocked, and emotional intelligence is treated as a fatal weakness. Your laws are less about governance and more about maintaining an illusion of superiority. The "Ministry of Accountability" exists not to enforce responsibility but to ensure that no one ever has to take the blame for anything. In Brotopia, freedom doesn't mean liberty for all; it means the freedom to avoid introspection, consequences, or growth.

Physically, Brotopia is a mess. The streets are lined with discarded fast-food wrappers because cleaning is considered beneath the alpha code. Gym equipment litters public spaces, most of it either broken or repurposed as makeshift furniture. Laundry piles up everywhere, with no one willing to take on what is perceived as "domestic labor." Public spaces are arenas for constant competition rather than collaboration, with every interaction devolving into a test of dominance. Instead of a thriving society, you've created a landscape of half-finished projects, abandoned responsibilities, and endless arguments over whose fault it is that nothing works.

At the heart of Brotopia's failure is its exclusionary ideology. The manosphere's vision of male solidarity quickly collapses under the weight of its own contradictions. Without women to scapegoat, the fractures within your society become impossible to ignore. Alphas clash over leadership, each one convinced of their own superiority. Sigmas refuse to participate, claiming they're too unique to conform. Betas are ostracized, relegated to the fringes of society as second-class citizens in a world that claims to value equality. The result is a society that tears itself apart, unable to function because everyone is too busy trying to prove their dominance. Instead of building something meaningful, you've constructed a fragile hierarchy that prioritizes competition over cooperation and posturing over progress.

The internal contradictions of Brotopia extend far beyond its governing principles. The manosphere's obsession with dominance means that even the most basic tasks become insurmountable challenges. Organizing resources, establishing infrastructure, and creating systems for public welfare all require collaboration, something that Brotopia fundamentally rejects. The result is a society that can't sustain itself, let alone thrive. Your refusal to acknowledge the value of traditionally "feminine" qualities like empathy, communication, and cooperation leaves you ill-equipped to address the complex challenges of running a community. Instead of solving problems, you double down on the very behaviors that created them, perpetuating a cycle of failure that leaves Brotopia perpetually on the brink of collapse.

What's most ironic about Brotopia is that it claims to represent freedom, yet it's defined by its rigid hierarchies and oppressive social norms. The very men who decry "cancel culture" and "woke politics" have created a society where stepping out of line means exile. Your so-called utopia is a place where individuality is punished unless it aligns with the alpha ideal, and where the pursuit of dominance stifles creativity, innovation, and personal growth. The freedom you claim to cherish is an illusion, replaced by a system that enforces conformity under the guise of strength. Far from being a beacon of liberty, Brotopia is a cautionary tale about the dangers of building a society on the fragile foundation of toxic masculinity.

Brotopia's failure isn't just a matter of logistics or ideology, it's a reflection of the deeper flaws in the manosphere's worldview. The fantasy of a male-only utopia reveals the extent to which your ideals are rooted in insecurity rather than strength. The exclusion of women isn't about creating a better society; it's about avoiding the challenges of equality and collaboration. The obsession with dominance isn't about empowerment; it's about compensating for a lack of self-worth. Brotopia isn't a testament to the power of masculinity, it's a monument to its fragility, a society that collapses under the weight of its own contradictions.

Despite its many failures, Brotopia remains a compelling fantasy for the manosphere because it offers a comforting escape from reality. It's a place where you don't have to confront your own shortcomings or reckon with the complexities of the modern world. Instead, you can retreat into a simplified narrative where your failures are someone else's fault and your successes are guaranteed by virtue of your gender. The appeal of Brotopia lies not in its promise of progress but in its ability to shield you from accountability. It's a utopia not of achievement but of avoidance, a society designed to validate your grievances rather than challenge you to grow.

The tragedy of Brotopia is that it could never succeed, not because of external forces but because of the internal contradictions that define it. A society that values dominance over cooperation, exclusion over inclusion, and posturing over substance is doomed to fail. The dream of Brotopia is a mirage, a fleeting vision of a perfect world that dissolves the moment you try to bring it into reality. It's a cautionary tale, a reminder that the ideals of the manosphere are not just flawed but fundamentally incompatible with the realities of building a functional society.

Ultimately, Brotopia is a reflection of the manosphere itself, a world built on fantasies and sustained by denial. It's a place where the pursuit of dominance leads to dysfunction, where the rejection of accountability leads to chaos, and where the obsession with power leads to isolation. The failure of Brotopia isn't just a failure of governance or ideology, it's a failure of imagination, a testament to what happens when you mistake strength for wisdom and arrogance for leadership. It's a world that could never exist, not because of external obstacles but because of the internal contradictions that define it. And as you look around at the wreckage of your so-called utopia, the question isn't why Brotopia failed, it's why you ever thought it could succeed.

Why Nothing Works in Brotopia

Brotopia's grand experiment in a male-only society descends into chaos with breathtaking speed, a testament to how little forethought went into its creation. The vision was bold: a utopia where men ruled supreme, freed from the so-called burdens imposed by women. The reality? A dysfunctional mess where the absence of women means the absence of essential skills, collaboration, and even the most rudimentary problem-solving abilities. What begins as a triumphant declaration of independence from feminism quickly devolves into a grim tableau of unwashed dishes, neglected infrastructure, and perpetual conflict. Brotopia proves, with brutal efficiency, that bravado and bluster cannot sustain a civilization.

Without women, Brotopia is stripped of the foundational skills that keep any society running smoothly. Cooking, cleaning, and conflict resolution, dismissed as unnecessary "feminine" traits, are glaringly absent. The kitchens of Brotopia are a horror show of charred protein pancakes, empty pizza boxes, and takeout containers, while the concept of cleaning is treated as an alien ritual. Laundry is abandoned, trash piles up, and even basic hygiene becomes a casualty of the manosphere's refusal to acknowledge the importance of domestic labor. The irony is as pungent as the unwashed gym clothes that litter the streets: for all their talk of being self-sufficient alphas, the men of Brotopia are utterly incapable of managing even the simplest of tasks without the support systems they so vehemently rejected.

The leadership vacuum compounds the chaos. In a society where every man believes he's the rightful alpha, governance becomes a farce. Town hall meetings devolve into shouting matches, with no one willing to compromise or cede authority. Cooperation is treated as weakness, and listening is derided as a beta trait. Every decision becomes a battle for dominance, leaving the community paralyzed by gridlock. Egos clash over trivial matters, and progress grinds to a halt because no one can agree on even the smallest course of action. In a place where power is the ultimate currency, leadership becomes a revolving door of posturing and backstabbing, with no one willing, or able, to provide genuine direction.

The physical infrastructure of Brotopia is a similarly bleak reflection of its dysfunction. The power grid fails repeatedly, plumbing backs up into chaos, and roads crumble into impassable hazards. The lack of practical skills among the population means that even the simplest repairs become insurmountable challenges. No one wants to undertake the "beta" work of maintenance, and the result is a society that is literally falling apart at the seams. When residents do attempt fixes, the efforts are haphazard and temporary, with the underlying issues left unresolved. Brotopia's refusal to value expertise or collaboration ensures that its physical systems are as fragile as its social ones. The result is a dystopian landscape of crumbling infrastructure and mounting frustrations, all of which could have been avoided if anyone had been willing to admit they didn't know everything.

The economy of Brotopia fares no better. In a society where dominance is the primary value, collaboration and innovation are nonexistent. The marketplace devolves into a primitive barter system where protein powder and energy drinks become the currency of choice. Long-term economic planning is abandoned in favor of immediate gratification, with business ventures collapsing under the weight of infighting and ego-driven decision-making. Partnerships dissolve over trivial disagreements, and any hope of innovation is quashed by the overwhelming need to assert superiority at all costs. The economy of Brotopia mirrors its broader culture: competitive to the point of self-destruction, incapable of meaningful growth, and wholly unsustainable.

Brotopia's failures aren't just amusing; they're a scathing indictment of the manosphere's values. Every breakdown, whether in leadership, infrastructure, or the economy, can be traced back to the same root cause: a refusal to embrace qualities like empathy, cooperation, and humility. These qualities, dismissed as weak or feminine, are essential for any functioning society. In their absence, Brotopia collapses under the weight of its own contradictions. The very traits its residents pride themselves on, self-reliance, dominance, and strength, prove utterly insufficient for building and sustaining a community. Instead of creating a utopia, they've built a monument to their own arrogance and short-sightedness.

The dysfunction extends beyond practical failures to the emotional and social fabric of Brotopia. Relationships, already strained by the hyper-competitive culture, disintegrate entirely as trust becomes an impossible commodity. Friendships are reduced to transactional alliances, and any sense of camaraderie is sacrificed at the altar of individualism. The absence of women, far from freeing men from perceived burdens, leaves a void that amplifies isolation and resentment. Brotopia becomes a breeding ground for bitterness, its residents trapped in a cycle of loneliness and misplaced blame. Instead of confronting their own shortcomings, they turn on one another, each man convinced that his neighbors are the true source of the community's failures.

The cultural landscape of Brotopia is equally bleak. Art, music, and literature, dismissed as frivolous or effeminate, are virtually nonexistent, leaving the community bereft of any creative or intellectual outlets. Entertainment is reduced to gym sessions and testosterone-fueled competitions, with no room for the exploration of ideas or emotions. The absence of cultural depth further entrenches the community's stagnation, robbing it of the very tools needed for reflection and growth. Brotopia's disdain for creativity ensures that its residents remain stuck in a shallow, repetitive cycle of consumption and aggression, unable to imagine a world beyond their immediate desires.

Brotopia's economy of dominance, its leadership vacuum, and its cultural stagnation all point to the same fundamental flaw: an unwillingness to embrace the qualities that make societies work. Cooperation, humility, and mutual respect are not weaknesses; they are the bedrock of civilization. Without them, Brotopia becomes a cautionary tale about the dangers of mistaking arrogance for strength and isolation for independence. It is a stark reminder that no society can thrive without a willingness to confront its own limitations and work together toward a common good. In rejecting these principles, Brotopia has not liberated its residents; it has trapped them in a prison of their own making.

The ultimate irony of Brotopia is that its failures were entirely predictable. The values that underpin it, dominance, individualism, and a rejection of perceived femininity, are inherently self-destructive. By refusing to value collaboration, empathy, or introspection, Brotopia ensures its own downfall. Its residents, convinced of their superiority, are blind to the very qualities that could save them. Instead of building a utopia, they have created a cautionary tale for the ages: a society that celebrates strength but cannot sustain itself, that prizes independence but collapses without cooperation, and that values dominance over all else but is ultimately dominated by its own flaws. Brotopia is not a triumph; it is a failure, and one that serves as a stark warning about the dangers of arrogance and the importance of humility.

The Downfall of Brotopia

The downfall of Brotopia is as inevitable as it is spectacular. For all its posturing as the ultimate male utopia, the cracks in its foundation start to show almost immediately, widening into a chasm of dysfunction that swallows the entire society whole. The experiment, which was supposed to prove that men could thrive without the "constraints" imposed by women or collaboration, quickly reveals itself to be a disaster of epic proportions. The very values that Brotopia was built on, dominance, hyper-individualism, and the rejection of so-called "weak" traits like empathy, become the seeds of its destruction.

Infighting becomes the defining feature of Brotopia. With every man vying for the coveted title of alpha, the community devolves into endless power struggles. Meetings intended to address the society's growing issues become battlegrounds of ego and bravado, with every participant more concerned with asserting dominance than solving problems. Disputes over leadership escalate from shouting matches to outright chaos, with alliances forming and dissolving in the blink of an eye. Without any willingness to compromise or work toward collective goals, the community spirals into gridlock. Every attempt at progress is derailed by the unrelenting need to "win," leaving Brotopia stuck in a perpetual state of dysfunction.

The infighting extends beyond leadership disputes. Day-to-day interactions in Brotopia are fraught with tension, as every encounter becomes a test of dominance. Friendships are strained by constant competition, and cooperation is dismissed as a sign of weakness. The result is a society where no one can trust anyone else, and every relationship is transactional at best. The dream of male solidarity that supposedly underpinned Brotopia is shattered by the reality of fragile egos and unchecked aggression. Instead of banding together to create a functional society, the residents of Brotopia tear each other apart, each man convinced that his neighbors are enemies to be outmaneuvered.

The system itself proves to be unsustainable. Hyper-individualism, celebrated as the cornerstone of Brotopia, quickly reveals its limitations. With every man focused solely on his own needs and desires, essential tasks go undone. Infrastructure collapses, and the community is left without the resources needed to sustain itself. Basic needs like food, shelter, and sanitation become insurmountable challenges because no one is willing to take on the "unmanly" work required to address them. The refusal to acknowledge or value these tasks ensures that Brotopia remains in a state of perpetual crisis. For all their talk of independence, the men of Brotopia are unable to function without the very systems they rejected.

The fragility of the system is further compounded by the residents' inability to confront their own limitations. Admitting a mistake or asking for help is seen as a sign of weakness, so problems are ignored or blamed on others. This refusal to take responsibility creates a feedback loop of dysfunction, where issues are never addressed and failures are never rectified. The society becomes a monument to denial, with every man clinging to the illusion of control even as the world around him crumbles. The contradictions that underpin Brotopia, hyper-individualism that necessitates cooperation, dominance that precludes humility, and strength that hides fragility, ensure its collapse.

Emotionally, Brotopia is a wasteland. The exclusionary nature of the society, which was supposed to create a utopia of male camaraderie, instead fosters isolation and insecurity. With no women to blame for their problems, the residents are forced to confront the uncomfortable reality that their issues are of their own making. The pressure to maintain the facade of strength takes an immense toll, leaving men emotionally hollow and deeply unhappy. But in a culture that values bravado over vulnerability, admitting to these feelings is unthinkable. The result is a community where everyone is miserable, but no one is willing to say it out loud.

The loneliness of Brotopia is palpable. Relationships, already strained by the hyper-competitive culture, become virtually nonexistent. The lack of meaningful connection leaves the residents adrift, each man trapped in his own bubble of self-interest and denial. The dream of a male-only utopia becomes a nightmare of isolation, with every man an island unto himself. The society that was supposed to free men from the perceived constraints of collaboration and empathy instead becomes a prison, built from their own insecurities and reinforced by their refusal to change.

Even the entertainment in Brotopia reflects its broader failures. Without creativity or cultural depth, the community's leisure activities are reduced to repetitive competitions and shallow distractions. The same cycles of dominance and posturing that define their society play out in their downtime, leaving no room for genuine enjoyment or fulfillment. The absence of art, music, and storytelling deprives Brotopia of the tools needed for introspection and growth, ensuring that its residents remain stuck in a shallow, stagnant existence.

The collapse of Brotopia is a microcosm of the manosphere's broader failures. It reveals, in stark detail, the consequences of a worldview that rejects cooperation, empathy, and introspection in favor of dominance and self-interest. The society that was supposed to prove the superiority of these values instead becomes a cautionary tale, illustrating their inherent flaws. Brotopia's downfall is not just a failure of logistics or leadership; it is a failure of ideology. The very principles that were supposed to make it strong instead make it weak, fragile, and unsustainable.

What is perhaps most tragic about Brotopia is that its failures were entirely avoidable. The qualities that its residents dismissed as weak, empathy, cooperation, and humility, are the very qualities that could have saved them. But their refusal to value these traits ensured that they were doomed from the start. Brotopia is not just a failed experiment; it is a reflection of the manosphere's broader inability to function in a world that requires collaboration and mutual respect. It serves as a stark reminder that no society can thrive without these principles, and that any attempt to build a utopia on their rejection is destined to fail.

Brotopia's downfall is as inevitable as it is tragic, a cautionary tale of hyper-individualism, fragile egos, and a refusal to embrace collaboration or empathy. Built on rejecting qualities deemed weak, this male-only "utopia" spirals into dysfunction, with power struggles, gridlocked leadership, and a society devoid of responsibility. Basic needs go unmet, relationships crumble under constant competition and isolation, and the dream of camaraderie collapses into a nightmare of loneliness and denial. For all its posturing about freedom, Brotopia becomes a prison, exposing the manosphere's failure to function in a world requiring cooperation and respect. The qualities dismissed as weak, empathy, effort, and introspection, could have saved it. Brotopia isn't just a failed experiment but a stark reflection of the manosphere's self-destructive values, warning that any society rejecting these principles is destined to crumble.

Chapter 12
The Silicon Savior Complex
Selling America for Spare Parts

The Rise of the Tech Bros

The rise of the tech bros is a cautionary tale of unchecked hubris masquerading as genius. These self-appointed saviors, armed with venture capital and an inflated sense of their own brilliance, have transformed themselves into modern-day monarchs, ruling not through democracy but through algorithms and profits. They promise innovation, efficiency, and solutions to humanity's problems but deliver a dystopian reality that thrives on greed and control. Under the guise of making the world "better," they've auctioned America off piece by piece, reducing public goods and democratic values into commodities for sale. Want clean water? That'll be $9.99 a month. Democracy? It's now a non-fungible token (NFT) with limited access. Privacy? Only available with a platinum subscription. These tech titans, celebrated for their disruptive brilliance, are nothing more than auctioneers, hawking the nation's soul to the highest bidder.

The tech bro mentality is defined by an insidious combination of greed and detachment. Problems are only worth solving if they can be monetized, and the solutions they offer are carefully crafted to create dependency, not empowerment. Public transportation is gutted in favor of app-based services that cater exclusively to affluent neighborhoods. Healthcare "innovations" are rolled out as premium services that prioritize profit margins over patient care. Even education, once a pillar of public good, is reduced to online courses that prioritize clicks and ad revenue over genuine learning. Everything becomes a subscription model, from the air we breathe to the rights we once took for granted. These tech bros have reimagined America as a pay-to-play society, where the wealthiest thrive while the rest are left scrambling for access to the basics.

Their obsession with algorithms only exacerbates the problem. These so-called solutions, touted as neutral and objective, are anything but. Algorithms amplify biases, exploit vulnerabilities, and create opaque systems that shield their creators from accountability. Hiring processes are gamed to exclude marginalized groups. Social media platforms optimize for outrage and division because it's profitable. Law enforcement uses predictive algorithms that disproportionately target communities of color. These systems don't make the world fairer or more efficient; they make it more exploitative and unequal. Yet the tech bros market them as progress, convincing us to trade our privacy, autonomy, and trust for convenience and efficiency. And as we hand over control, they tighten their grip, creating systems designed not to serve humanity but to serve their bottom line.

This dystopian landscape doesn't just harm individuals, it reshapes the cultural and political fabric of society, often in ways that align disturbingly well with the manosphere's toxic ideology. The tech bros and the manosphere share a common language of dominance, control, and grievance. Both thrive on the promise of restoring power to those who feel it has been unfairly taken from them. The tech bros, under the guise of innovation, create tools and platforms that amplify the manosphere's reach, turning toxic ideas into viral movements. Algorithms prioritize incendiary content, ensuring that misogynistic rants and conspiracy theories reach millions. Social media platforms provide echo chambers where the manosphere's ideas can fester and grow, unchecked by reality or accountability.

But the connection between the tech bros and the manosphere goes deeper than mere amplification. It's a symbiotic relationship where the tech bros manipulate the manosphere for their own gain. By providing platforms that fuel the grievances of disaffected men, they create a loyal user base that keeps scrolling, clicking, and consuming. The manosphere's influencers sell the dream of alpha dominance, but the tech bros sell the tools to chase it: dating apps designed to gamify relationships, fitness trackers marketed as essential to achieving the "ideal" male physique, and crypto platforms that promise wealth and independence but deliver little more than financial instability. Every click, every like, every subscription feeds into a system designed to extract maximum value from the very men who believe they're fighting against the system.

The tech bros don't just enable the manosphere, they exploit it. They use its rhetoric of freedom and independence to mask their own agendas, turning disaffected men into unwitting pawns in a broader game of power and profit. While the manosphere rails against the so-called tyranny of feminism and "woke culture," the tech bros quietly reshape public policy, often with the backing of billionaire investors who have their own regressive agendas. These investors pour money into platforms that spread misinformation and division, knowing full well that a fractured, angry population is easier to control. The manosphere becomes a convenient distraction, a way to keep the public focused on cultural grievances while the tech bros auction off the nation's resources and liberties behind closed doors.

The Silicon Savior Complex, the belief that tech bros are uniquely qualified to solve society's problems, is perhaps their most dangerous myth. It allows them to operate without scrutiny, turning their greed into genius and their exploitation into innovation. But the reality is far less flattering. Their obsession with profit blinds them to the human cost of their actions. Their algorithms erode trust and deepen inequality. Their platforms fuel division and undermine democracy. And their rhetoric of disruption and efficiency masks a reality where nothing is truly fixed, only sold, resold, and commodified until there's nothing left.

The question isn't whether the tech bros are saving the world. It's whether we can afford to let them keep pretending they are. Their vision of the future, a world governed by algorithms, subscriptions, and the whims of billionaire investors, isn't just dystopian. It's dangerous. It's a world where public goods are privatized, democracy is an afterthought, and the very concept of community is reduced to a series of transactions. It's a world where freedom is just another product to be bought and sold, and those who can't afford it are left behind.

For the manosphere, this partnership with the tech bros feels like a validation of their grievances, a way to project their ideology onto a global stage. But in reality, it's a betrayal. The tech bros aren't empowering the manosphere, they're exploiting it, using its followers as pawns in a larger game of greed and control. The promise of alpha dominance, financial independence, and cultural relevance is a lie, designed to keep the manosphere engaged and consuming. The real winners aren't the men chasing these dreams, they're the tech bros selling them.

The rise of the tech bros and their Silicon Savior Complex isn't just a cautionary tale about greed and hubris. It's a reflection of how easily power can be consolidated when no one is paying attention. It's a warning about the dangers of unchecked innovation, where the drive for profit overrides any consideration of ethics or humanity. And it's a call to action, a reminder that if we don't challenge their narrative, we risk losing not just our public goods and democratic values but our very ability to imagine a better future.

The manosphere and the tech bros may seem like separate phenomena, but they're deeply intertwined, feeding off each other's rhetoric and reinforcing each other's worst tendencies. Together, they create a culture that glorifies dominance, devalues empathy, and prioritizes profit over people. It's a culture that promises freedom but delivers exploitation, a world where the only winners are those at the very top. And as long as we let them dictate the terms, we're all complicit in building the very dystopia they claim to be saving us from.

Living in the Subscription Economy

Living in the subscription economy engineered by tech bros is like being stuck in a dystopian theme park where every ride requires a separate fee, and the exits are intentionally hard to find. The cost of basic human needs, once fundamental rights or public services has been transformed into a recurring charge that siphons wealth upward while leaving everyone else scrambling to make ends meet. Healthcare is no longer about healing; it's about profit. Want access to life-saving treatments? That's a premium package. Education, once the great equalizer, is now an exclusive club where quality learning is locked behind paywalls, leaving public institutions underfunded and crumbling. Even public infrastructure, from roads to clean water, has been sliced into segments and auctioned off to the highest bidder. Everything comes with a subscription fee, and the only guarantee is that prices will go up while quality plummets. The tech bros have turned society into a monetized game where the winners are those who own the rules.

The manosphere, naturally, buys into this distorted vision, seeing it as an extension of their grievances against a world they feel has left them behind. The rhetoric of "individual freedom" and "anti-elite rebellion" that the manosphere preaches aligns disturbingly well with the tech bro vision of a fragmented society where everyone fights for scraps while the powerful consolidate control. The irony, of course, is that the manosphere's followers are the first to suffer under these systems. The subscription economy doesn't care about their imagined alpha status, it's designed to extract as much as possible from them while giving as little as necessary in return. Whether it's overpriced fitness apps marketed to insecure men or exclusive dating platforms that promise access to "high-value" partners, the tech bro ecosystem preys on the very insecurities the manosphere amplifies.

The illusion of free speech perpetuated by tech platforms is another cornerstone of this dystopia. Tech bros market their platforms as havens for open discourse, claiming they provide space for all voices to be heard. But in reality, free speech under their watch is selectively enforced based on profit margins and political expediency. Content that generates outrage and engagement is prioritized, while genuine discourse is buried under a deluge of algorithms designed to maximize clicks. The manosphere thrives in this environment, where toxic ideas and incendiary rhetoric are rewarded with visibility, not because they're insightful, but because they're profitable. The tech bros profit from the chaos, turning every misogynistic rant and every conspiratorial video into ad revenue. Meanwhile, voices calling for genuine equality or nuanced discussion are drowned out, shadow banned, or flagged as "controversial" because they don't fit the profit-driven narrative.

The manosphere, for all its talk of rebellion and anti-establishment values, is a willing pawn in this system. Its influencers and followers feed the algorithm with their rage and grievances, ensuring that the cycle continues. Every click on a video about "the feminist agenda," every share of a post decrying "cancel culture," and every like on a meme mocking women adds fuel to the tech bro machine. The manosphere becomes both the product and the consumer, trapped in a feedback loop that enriches its puppet masters while keeping it convinced of its own autonomy. The tech bros have built a system where outrage is the currency, and the manosphere is their most reliable ATM.

Privacy, once a cornerstone of freedom, has been obliterated in the process. The tech bro empire runs on data, and every click, swipe, and purchase feeds their insatiable appetite for user information. They don't just sell you products; they sell you. Your preferences, habits, and insecurities are packaged and auctioned off to the highest bidder, creating a surveillance economy where every move you make is monitored, monetized, and manipulated. The manosphere, with its penchant for performative rebellion, rails against perceived invasions of privacy by governments or feminists but turns a blind eye to the tech bros siphoning their data to fund targeted ads and curated content designed to keep them scrolling. The real invader isn't some shadowy conspiracy, it's the algorithm serving them another video about why modern women are the root of all problems.

The subscription economy doesn't just extract wealth; it extracts agency. When every aspect of life is controlled by paywalls and terms of service, the ability to make meaningful choices is eroded. You don't get to decide what content you see, what options you have, or even how you interact with the world, those decisions are made for you by algorithms designed to prioritize profit over people. The manosphere's followers, for all their talk of independence and dominance, are some of the most controlled and manipulated individuals in this system. Their feeds are curated to amplify their fears and insecurities, ensuring they remain engaged and enraged. Their choices are limited to the options presented by platforms that don't have their best interests at heart. And their voices, far from being amplified, are commodified and exploited.

The manosphere and the tech bro empire are two sides of the same coin, each feeding off the other to sustain their own flawed systems. The manosphere provides the outrage, the engagement, and the blind loyalty that the tech bros need to keep their platforms profitable. In return, the tech bros provide the tools, the spaces, and the algorithms that allow the manosphere to grow and thrive. It's a symbiotic relationship built on exploitation and greed, where the only winners are the ones pulling the strings. The subscription economy, with its promise of convenience and personalization, is just another layer of control in a system designed to keep you compliant and consuming.

The cost of living in this economy isn't just financial, it's cultural, social, and psychological. It erodes trust, deepens divides, and perpetuates a cycle of dependency that benefits the few at the expense of the many. It turns society into a marketplace, where every interaction is transactional and every relationship is reduced to a series of clicks and swipes. And it leaves you trapped, scrolling through a curated feed of grievances and promises, never realizing that the system isn't designed to empower you, it's designed to exploit you. The subscription economy isn't just a business model; it's a way of life that strips you of your humanity while convincing you that you're in control. And until you recognize that, you'll remain a pawn in a game you didn't even know you were playing.

The Hollow Future They Built

The hollow future built by tech bros is a testament to what happens when progress is divorced from humanity, and innovation is driven solely by profit. In their race to disrupt every industry and solve problems no one asked them to fix, tech bros have created a fractured, inequitable, and compassionless dystopia. Their focus has never been on building a better world but on constructing systems that prioritize control, commodification, and their own financial gain. The result is a society where human connections are replaced by algorithms, where inequality isn't just a byproduct but a feature, and where the very fabric of community is unraveling. For all their talk of shaping the future, what they've created is a world that benefits a select few at the expense of everyone else.

The myth of the Silicon Savior, a genius billionaire who will lead us to a utopian future, has become one of the most damaging narratives of our time. Figures like Elon Musk, Jeff Bezos, and Mark Zuckerberg are elevated to near-deity status, their flaws ignored, and their failures reframed as stepping stones to greatness. This cult of personality doesn't just excuse their mistakes; it shields them from accountability. They're hailed as visionaries even as their decisions deepen societal divides, erode trust in institutions, and undermine democratic principles. The manosphere, naturally, idolizes these tech bros, seeing them as proof that dominance and individualism can lead to success. But the reality is that these so-called saviors aren't building a future for everyone; they're building a future for themselves. Their innovations aren't designed to uplift humanity, they're designed to extract as much value as possible while leaving the rest of the world to deal with the fallout.

And what is the real cost of this greed? It's not just measured in dollars but in lives and opportunities lost. The rise of the gig economy, fueled by tech platforms, has left countless workers trapped in precarious jobs with no benefits, no stability, and no path forward. Environmental degradation accelerates as these companies prioritize convenience and growth over sustainability, wrapping their destruction in hollow promises of green initiatives. Communities are left hollowed out as local economies are disrupted, and small businesses are crushed under the weight of global monopolies. And yet, the tech bros shrug off these consequences, treating them as inevitable side effects of progress. They've created a world where the human toll of their so-called innovations is ignored, swept under the rug of profitability and wrapped in the veneer of progress.

The manosphere's connection to this dystopia is undeniable. The same toxic ideals that drive the manosphere, hyper-individualism, a disdain for accountability, and an obsession with dominance, are mirrored in the ethos of the tech industry. Tech bros and manosphere influencers share a symbiotic relationship, feeding off each other's rhetoric and reinforcing each other's worldview. The tech industry provides the platforms and algorithms that amplify manosphere content, turning outrage into engagement and engagement into revenue. In return, the manosphere gives tech bros a loyal audience of consumers eager to buy into their vision of the future. It's a cycle of mutual exploitation, where both parties profit from the same system of control and commodification.

This future of control isn't just theoretical, it's already here. Algorithms dictate what you see, hear, and even think, shaping your perception of reality without your consent. Every click, every swipe, and every search feeds into a system designed to predict and manipulate your behavior. The manosphere thrives in this environment, using the same tools of control to spread its message and build its following. But this isn't empowerment, it's entrapment. The tech industry and the manosphere claim to offer freedom, but what they're really selling is a cage. It's a world where your value is measured in data points and your choices are limited to what the algorithm decides to show you.

The emotional toll of living in this hollow future cannot be overstated. Isolation and disconnection become the norm as human relationships are replaced by transactional interactions and digital substitutes. The manosphere feeds on this loneliness, offering its followers a sense of belonging while deepening their insecurities and grievances. But this sense of belonging is hollow, built on a foundation of mutual resentment and mistrust. It's not a community, it's a trap, designed to keep its members angry, isolated, and engaged. And for all its talk of rebellion and freedom, the manosphere is as much a product of the tech bro dystopia as the algorithms it decries.

This dystopia's failures extend beyond its emotional and social toll to its inability to deliver on its promises of innovation and progress. The systems built by tech bros are brittle, riddled with contradictions, and designed to benefit the few at the expense of the many. Their solutions often create more problems than they solve, leaving society to pick up the pieces while they move on to their next venture. The manosphere mirrors this pattern, offering shallow solutions to complex problems and leaving its followers more disillusioned and disconnected than before. Both systems thrive on the illusion of empowerment while stripping away the very tools needed for genuine growth and progress.

As the tech industry and the manosphere continue to shape our world, the question becomes not just what kind of future they're building, but whether that future is one we want to live in. A society built on greed, control, and exclusion cannot stand. The qualities dismissed by both the tech bros and the manosphere, empathy, cooperation, and accountability, are the very qualities needed to build a sustainable and equitable future. Without them, their systems are destined to crumble under the weight of their own contradictions, leaving nothing but chaos and division in their wake.

The future brought to us by tech bros isn't one of freedom or innovation but one of control and commodification. It's a future where every aspect of life is monitored, monetized, and manipulated for profit, leaving no room for humanity or connection. The manosphere, as both a product and a participant in this system, serves as a stark reminder of what happens when toxic ideals are allowed to flourish unchecked. Both the tech industry and the manosphere claim to offer solutions, but what they really provide is a reflection of our society's deepest flaws. The hollow future they've built isn't just a cautionary tale, it's a call to action. Without humanity at its core, even the most "brilliant" systems are doomed to fail.

Feel Free to Draw a Tiny Picture of Your Tiny Soul Below

Public Service Announcement
Touché Tiki Torches
White Supremacy for Fits & Giggles

The Uniform of the Fragile Ego

The image of angry men in khakis and polo shirts, brandishing Tiki torches, is both absurd and unsettling. Is it a hate rally or a misguided backyard barbecue? This uniform, the unspoken dress code of modern white supremacy, mirrors the fragile bravado of the manosphere. Both movements try to project power while clinging to aesthetics that scream respectability and control. The khakis and polos are no accident. They sanitize the ideology, masking hate with a suburban, middle-class facade meant to say, "We're just ordinary guys defending our rights." But the act is as transparent as the manosphere's attempts to cloak insecurity in grindset memes and alpha rhetoric.

Then come the Tiki torches, absurdly appropriated from backyard patios to serve as symbols of menace. These flimsy, plastic props highlight the impotence of a movement desperate to appear strong while wielding tools better suited for warding off mosquitoes. Much like the manosphere's motivational soundbites, the torches are props in a performance of power that collapses under scrutiny. There's no substance behind the flames, only fragile egos clinging to the illusion of dominance.

The overlap between white supremacy and the manosphere isn't coincidental. Both are fueled by fear, fear of losing status, of equality, of a world where dominance isn't guaranteed. Both thrive on the same grievances, painting themselves as victims of progress while railing against imagined oppressors. The fury isn't about defending values; it's about preserving privilege and resisting change. Strip away the khakis and extinguish the torches, and what's left is the same fragile ego that shouts about alpha dominance while blaming everyone else for its failures.

Whether marching under Tiki torches or posting on social media, it's the same tantrum in a different costume, proving once again that fragile masculinity fuels both movements in equal measure.

The Khaki-Powered Crusade

The so-called "khaki-powered crusade" is a perfect extension of the manosphere's insecurities, marching forward with grievances as hollow as they are absurd. Why are they out there? Because their imagined world of unchallenged dominance is crumbling, and nothing terrifies them more than equality or the possibility of losing their place at the top of a hierarchy that exists only in their minds. The same fear of "replacement" that fuels white supremacy mirrors the manosphere's obsession with a mythical past when men ruled without question and everyone else knew their "place." Whether it's diversity, feminism, or basic human decency, they frame progress as an existential threat to their fragile sense of self.

The khakis and polos aren't just a uniform; they're a desperate attempt to package their insecurities as power. Like the manosphere's grindset gurus and alpha influencers, these marches project a facade of strength while exposing their glaring weakness. How strong can you be if your entire identity shatters at the idea of someone else sharing space at the table? The spectacle of preppy rage isn't dominance, it's desperation in a costume. Their chants and torches don't signal power; they scream fear.

Social media and manosphere forums amplify their grievances into collective hysteria. Echo chambers radicalize participants, feeding them a toxic stew of groupthink and conspiracy theories that turn personal insecurities into public spectacles. Like bro influencers spouting grindset ideology, the white supremacist marches aren't about real change but performative outrage. These demonstrations are just another stage for their tantrums, an attention-grab dressed up as activism. It's the same playbook: loud, shallow, and completely devoid of introspection. Together, they form a feedback loop of entitlement and rage, where the real goal isn't progress but a desperate attempt to avoid confronting their own failures.

The Legacy of Laughable Hate

The aftermath of the khaki-clad marches is as predictable as it is humiliating. For all their chants, torches, and posturing, these public displays of hate often collapse under the weight of their absurdity. Videos of men marching with Tiki torches become viral memes, turning their so-called movement into a laughingstock overnight. Employers fire them, families disown them, and society reacts with well-earned backlash. Far from advancing their cause, these events often serve to discredit their ideology, exposing it for what it truly is: a fragile temper tantrum dressed up as a crusade. The manosphere might cheer these antics from behind their keyboards, but even they can't deny the overwhelming public humiliation that follows.

White supremacy, like the manosphere, has become a losing brand. For all their claims of strength and dominance, these marches reduce their ideology to a farcical sideshow. The khakis, polos, and Tiki torches, symbols meant to evoke power, only highlight their mediocrity. They project an image of control while revealing a movement built on fear, insecurity, and bad fashion choices. Even their supporters must grapple with the optics of their antics: how can anyone take seriously a group of men whose idea of rebellion looks more like a poorly planned barbecue than a revolution? In their attempt to intimidate, they inspire ridicule, eroding their cause with every march that ends in viral mockery.

The comedy of cowardice lies at the heart of their efforts. These men claim to fight for strength and dominance but cower behind pseudo-intellectual rhetoric, cherry-picked statistics, and vague historical references. Like the manosphere influencers they idolize, their arguments are shallow, their logic flimsy, and their bravery nonexistent. Their marches are not a call to action but a performance of outrage, designed to draw attention to themselves rather than enact meaningful change. They scream about courage while hiding behind their sanitized uniforms, too afraid to confront the real complexities of the world they live in.

What makes this spectacle even more ridiculous is the sheer mediocrity of their presentation. The khaki-and-polo ensemble is less a symbol of unity and more a bland declaration of conformity. Their chants are uninspired, their slogans recycled, and their torches, originally meant to illuminate, become the perfect metaphor for their dim understanding of the world. For a group so obsessed with dominance, their aesthetic is laughably weak, a reflection of an ideology that can't even intimidate without borrowing props from Home Depot.

Their legacy is one of laughable hate, a stark reminder that toxic ideologies collapse under their contradictions. If this is what supremacy looks like, it's time to rethink the branding, or the pants. Their actions reflect the themes of this book: fragile worldviews masquerading as strength, destined to fall apart in the face of progress. The connection to the manosphere is undeniable; both thrive on insecurity disguised as dominance, feeding on resentment and fear of change. Like khaki-clad marchers with Tiki torches, the manosphere clings to outdated notions of masculinity, desperate to project strength while exposing vulnerabilities. Their obsession with control, over women, minorities, or dissenters, reveals a hollow ideology fueled by anger and regression. The real question isn't why they march, podcast, or churn out grindset videos, but why anyone follows leaders offering nothing of value. Spoiler: it's not for the logic. It's the appeal of belonging to a group where insecurity is validated, accountability avoided, and failure conveniently blamed on others. Both the Tiki-torch bearers and manosphere influencers promise empowerment but deliver isolation and irrelevance.

Feel Free to Draw Yourself Loved and Giving Love Below

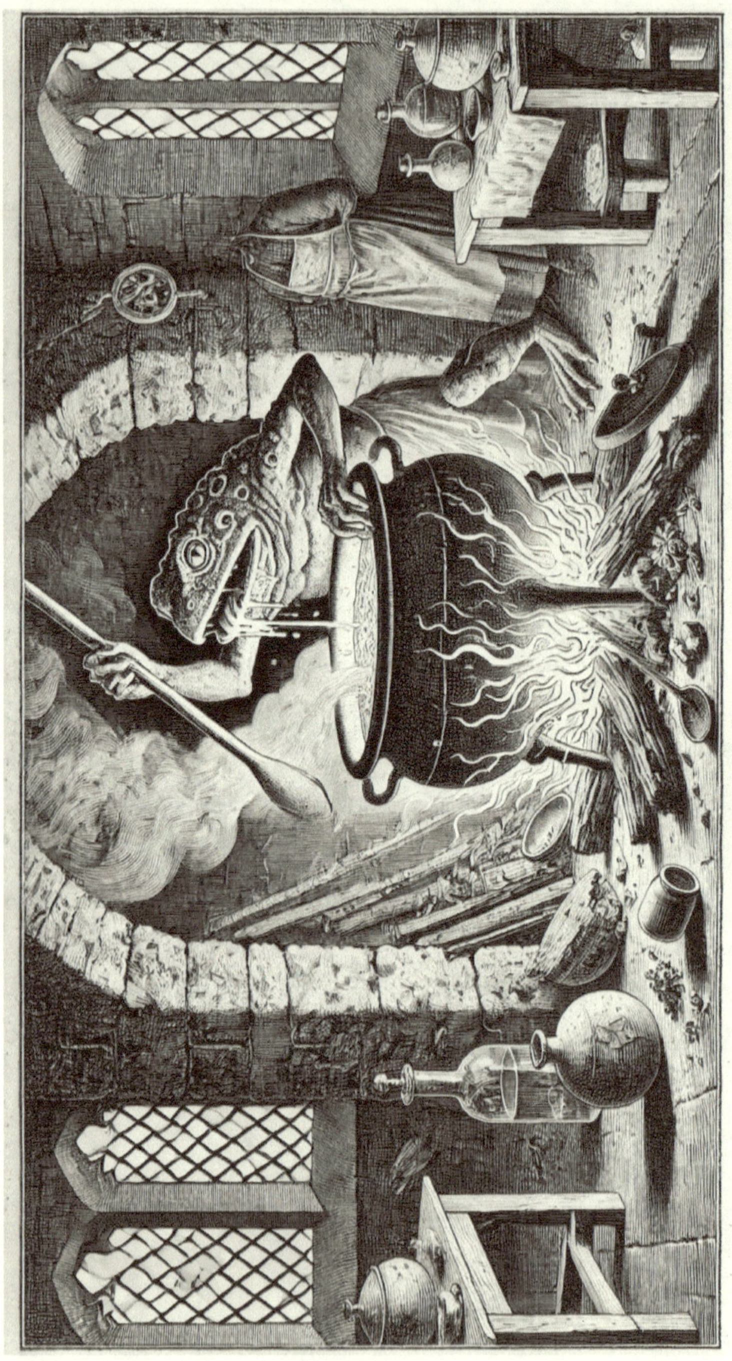

Bonus Chapter
Frog Juice – Utter Bile is Your Vile Vial, Please Don't Choke On it

What's in the Bro Brew?
The manosphere's drink of choice, "Frog Juice Bro Brew," is a vile concoction that you can't help but chug, even as it leaves you gagging. It's not real juice, of course, but a metaphorical cocktail brewed from conspiracy theories, toxic masculinity, and pure bile. Every sip reinforces your worldview, even if the aftertaste is unbearable. Why seek enlightenment or self-reflection when you can drown your insecurities in a brew that tells you everything wrong with your life is someone else's fault? It's the drink of champions, if the championship you're vying for is self-destruction.

So, what's in the Bro Brew? Its primary ingredient is fear, fear of progress, fear of change, fear that your carefully constructed façade of dominance is crumbling under the weight of a world that refuses to cater to your insecurities. Next comes disdain for empathy, because vulnerability is weakness, and showing compassion is akin to surrender. Then there's the obsession with dominance, a heaping dose of paranoia, and a splash of performative bravado to mask the bitterness. Stir it all together, and you've got a drink potent enough to keep you perpetually stunted, emotionally and intellectually. The flavor profile is as predictable as it is nauseating: a bitter blend of blame, self-pity, and denial. You sip it, choking on every gulp, but you can't seem to stop because the alternative, facing reality, is unthinkable.

Consuming this toxic worldview doesn't nourish you; it leaves you gagging on your own rhetoric. The more you drink, the more you're trapped in a cycle of regurgitating the same tired talking points. Every conversation, online or off, becomes an opportunity to spew bile about feminism, cancel culture, or the mythical war on men. You can't even enjoy your gains at the gym without spiraling into a rant about how society doesn't value "real men" anymore. The Bro Brew doesn't hydrate; it dehydrates, sapping you of reason, compassion, and perspective. Yet, you keep sipping, convinced it's the secret to alpha supremacy.

The manosphere's rhetoric is essentially a poorly mixed cocktail of bad ideas, and even you struggle to swallow it. Picture this: forums and social media act as your local dive bar, serving bottom-shelf conspiracy theories with a garnish of pseudo-intellectualism. Podcasts are the bartenders, mixing up custom blends of grindset sermons and misogynistic rants tailored to your tastes. Influencers are the snake oil salesmen, bottling this poison and selling it as self-improvement. And you, the loyal customer, line up every day for your fix, ignoring the fact that every sip makes you lonelier, angrier, and less equipped to handle the world.

The manosphere's echo chambers function as toxic breweries. In these spaces, bad takes are stirred with even worse solutions, creating an environment where the only voices heard are those that reinforce your worst instincts. Algorithms amplify this noise, ensuring that every post, comment, or video you consume further entrenches you in the ideology. The result is a perfectly curated experience designed to make you feel justified in your bitterness and validated in your victimhood. It's not just a drink, it's a lifestyle, one that leaves you isolated from meaningful connections and incapable of growth.

The side effects of sipping Bro Brew are as predictable as the ingredients. Isolation becomes your default state because the worldview you've adopted alienates you from everyone who doesn't share it. Bitterness seeps into every aspect of your life, from your relationships to your career, leaving you resentful and stuck. Even the influencers you idolize can't stomach their own brew, doubling down on performative bravado to mask their discomfort. They project an image of strength and success, but behind the scenes, they're as miserable as the audience they exploit. The taste test doesn't lie: this concoction is toxic, even for those who profit from it.

And yet, you keep drinking. Why? Because the brew promises answers, even if they're the wrong ones. It tells you that your failures aren't your fault, they're the result of a rigged system, feminists, or society at large. It gives you an excuse to avoid accountability, to blame others instead of examining your own choices. It's comforting in its simplicity, even as it poisons your potential for growth. The brew doesn't solve your problems; it numbs you to them, leaving you perpetually stuck in a cycle of frustration and denial.

But let's talk about the cost of this vile vial. Drinking Bro Brew doesn't just harm you, it harms everyone around you. Your relationships suffer as you push away anyone who challenges your worldview. Your financial stability crumbles because grindset culture prioritizes quick fixes over long-term planning. Your mental health deteriorates as bitterness and paranoia take root, leaving you more isolated and insecure than ever. The brew doesn't empower you; it breaks you, piece by piece, until all that's left is a hollow shell of the person you could have been.

There is a way out, but it requires facing your fears and taking responsibility. Spitting out the brew means rejecting lies, embracing vulnerability, and leaving behind echo chambers and self-proclaimed gurus. It's not easy, but it's the only way to break free. Most of you won't; the brew's promises are too addictive, even as they destroy you. Continuing to drink poisons not just you but the world around you, perpetuating fear, anger, and division. So here's your final warning: put down the vial before it drags you further into the void. The choice is yours, escape or drown.

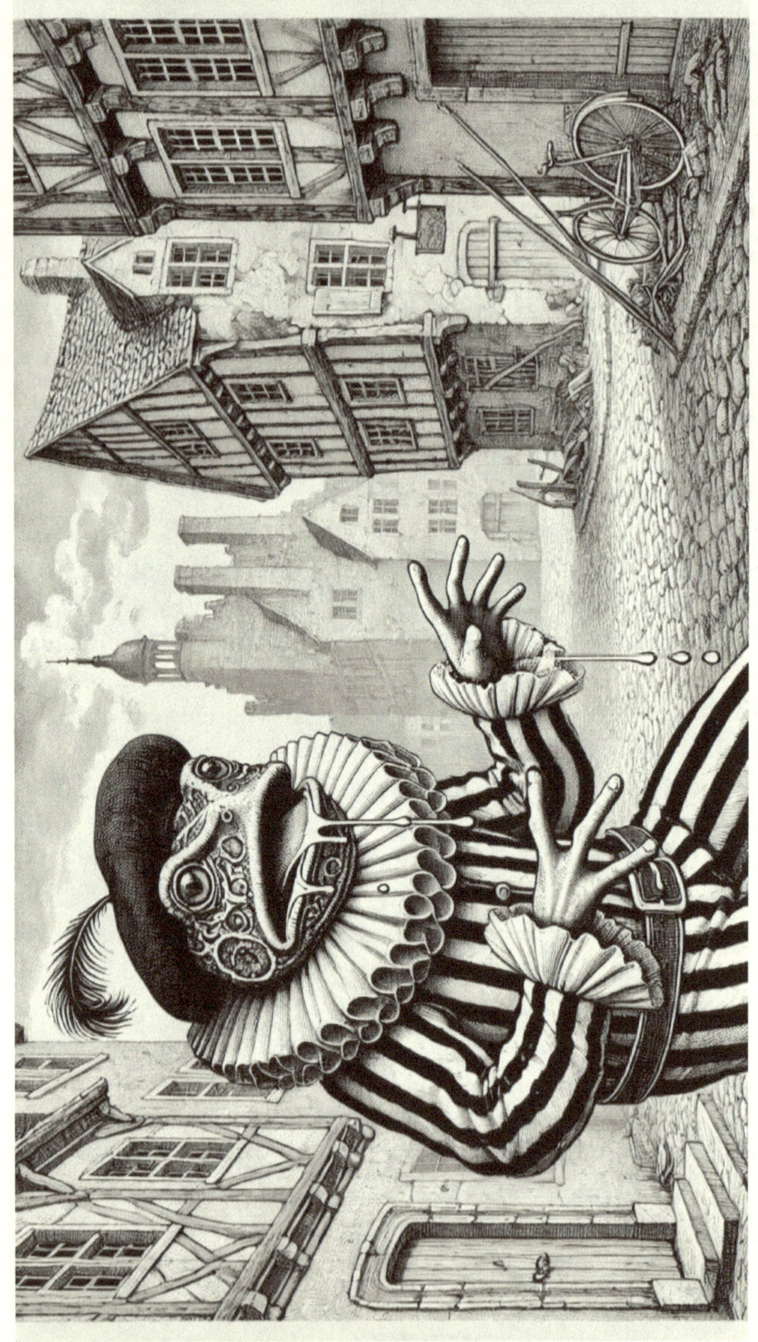

In Closing
Finally, You 'Guys' Are So Boring
Laughing Through the Bro Tears

A World of Your Own Making

Congratulations, bro, you've done it. You got everything you ever wanted. Feminism has been vanquished, social progress erased, and your hyper-masculine, patriarchal utopia reigns supreme. Yet, somehow, you're still miserable. Strange how that works. The world you demanded, a place where women are subjugated, individuality is crushed under the grindset, and "traditional values" reign, is here, and yet you're crying into your protein shake about how unfair it all feels. Maybe, just maybe, the problem isn't women, feminism, or cancel culture. Maybe the common denominator in all your misery is, well, you.

The reality is that it was never about the world around you. It was about your inability to adapt, to grow, or to take even a modicum of accountability for your choices. This book has dissected your fragile ecosystem: your toxic masculinity masquerading as strength, your performative dominance, your economic absurdities, and your unrelenting ego. You tore down progress and replaced it with a system built in your image, and now you hate what you see. The irony would be funny if it weren't so pathetic. You are the creator of your own unhappiness, the architect of a society so riddled with your own insecurities that it can't help but implode. This isn't the world feminism built, it's the one you did. Congratulations on the masterpiece.

It's a strange thing, isn't it, to look around and realize you've trapped yourself? But instead of acknowledging the root causes, your fear of change, your resentment of vulnerability, your obsession with control, you double down. You've been sold a worldview that promised empowerment but delivered isolation. You chased dominance at the expense of connection, mistaking control for fulfillment. Now, here you are, sitting atop your throne of grievance and wondering why it all feels so hollow. The punchline? The systems you championed have turned against you. Your economy of resentment only perpetuates your misery, your echo chambers amplify your insecurities, and the people you idolize profit off your despair while offering nothing of real value. The ultimate irony is that you've built a world where you can't even stand yourself.

When everything around you is crumbling, what's left? Laughter, apparently. Gallows humor becomes your final defense mechanism because the alternative, facing reality, is unbearable. It's easier to laugh at your self-inflicted dystopia than to fix it. And oh, the jokes write themselves. Your endless complaints about cancel culture while wielding your own brand of cancellation against anyone who dares challenge you. Your obsession with "traditional values" while failing to embody anything remotely resembling integrity. Your glorification of dominance as your entire identity collapses under its contradictions. The memes are funny, bro, but the tears you shed are even better. You've become a parody of yourself, whining about the systems you helped create, pretending that doubling down on bad ideas will somehow fix them.

The world you envisioned, one of unchecked hyper-masculinity, dominance, and rigid hierarchy, is falling apart. It was never sustainable because it was built on fear, insecurity, and lies. Your heroes, those so-called alpha influencers, sold you a dream of supremacy while cashing in on your desperation. Your utopia doesn't work because it isn't based on cooperation, empathy, or humility. It's a fragile house of cards, and every gust of reality sends it tumbling. The systems you thought would lift you up are the same ones crushing you under their weight. And yet, you keep sipping the brew, gagging on its bile but refusing to spit it out because admitting it's poison would mean admitting you've been wrong all along.

So what now? There's a path forward, but let's be honest, you probably won't take it. It requires you to do something that terrifies you: take responsibility and embrace change. It means stepping out of your echo chambers, rejecting the toxic rhetoric you've been sold, and doing the hard work of self-improvement. It means realizing that the real enemy isn't feminism, cancel culture, or any external factor, it's your own refusal to grow. But growth is hard, and blame is easy. Most of you will stick with what's comfortable, doubling down on your grievances and perpetuating the cycle of misery. Why change when you can stay in your bubble, surrounded by people who validate your worst impulses?

And that's the saddest part. You could have so much more. You could build real connections, foster genuine strength, and contribute to a world that values humanity over dominance. Instead, you cling to a broken ideology that promises the world and delivers nothing. The influencers you follow, the systems you support, and the values you champion aren't lifting you up, they're dragging you down. But hey, at least you have your memes, right? The gallows humor might not fix anything, but it sure takes the edge off as you watch your world crumble.

In the end, you got what you wanted, and it still wasn't enough. Maybe the problem was never the world, it was always you. But hey, thanks for the laughs. Your theatrics have been entertaining, if nothing else. As the world moves on without you, the rest of us will be here, chuckling at the absurdity of it all. After all, if you're not going to learn from your mistakes, the least we can do is enjoy the show.

Feel Free to Draw a Tiny Picture of Your Tiny Tears Below

Yes, We Are Laughing at You

Yes, we kind of hate you now.
Why wouldn't we hate our oppressors?
You hold the whip,
Yet complain your hand is sore.
You build the cage,
Then cry that it's lonely inside.

You shout, "Men Too!" as if oppressed,
A ridiculous rallying cry,
From the ones who locked the doors
And swallowed the keys.
Do you not hear the absurdity?
The echo of your grievance ricochets,
A hollow sound in a hollow cause.

Your kingdoms of dust choke the air,
Your victories ring empty in the void.
You bemoan a world you dismantled yourself,
Brick by brick,
While blaming us for the rubble.

Yes, we hate you for what you've done,
But hate alone cannot carry us.
So we laugh,
Because you make it so easy.
Because your "struggles" are a satire
You wrote and forgot was fiction.

Men Too? Really?
The oppressors demanding pity
Is the punchline no one could write better.
So yes, we laugh at you,
But only because it keeps us from screaming.
Only because your downfall is inevitable,
And the jokes will outlast your rule.

To Non-Manosphere Readers: A Warning

If you've made it this far, consider yourself armed with an invaluable guide for navigating the treacherous waters of the manosphere. Let this serve as a clear warning: stay far away from these pretenders. The men of the manosphere may package their ideology as empowerment or self-improvement, but beneath the surface lies a toxic swamp of insecurity, manipulation, and deception. They sell you strength, dominance, and success while masking a deep fragility that thrives on resentment. Their world isn't about building men up, it's about tearing everyone else down.

For men, these movements promise brotherhood but deliver isolation, dressing up emotional immaturity and entitlement as masculinity. The personas they idolize, grindset gurus, alpha influencers, bro podcasters, aren't role models. They're opportunists exploiting your insecurities for clicks, likes, and profit. Their version of masculinity isn't freedom; it's a cage of unreachable standards, performative toughness, and hollow victories. Walk away before you lose yourself to their echo chambers of anger and self-destruction.

For women, the warning is just as urgent. These ideologies aim to undermine your autonomy, dismiss your humanity, and reduce you to an object of conquest or blame. The more attention these pretenders receive, the more emboldened they become to push harmful narratives and policies that strip away equality. Protect your energy, call out their behavior when safe, and refuse to validate their rhetoric, in real life or online. The manosphere thrives on division, preying on fear, insecurity, and ignorance. Reject their bait. Seek role models and communities that foster empathy, growth, and respect. The antidote to their toxicity is simple: humanity. Choose it, choose a better path.

Esme Mees & Biddie Beuys, Winter 2025

List of Prints

About EATMS Productions

What's happening to women now is not random. It's structural.

Policy, culture, technology, and power are moving in the same direction.

EATMS maps them clearly and shows how to respond.

This title is part of an ongoing body of work. All EATMS Productions titles, across all series, authors, and formats, are components of a single connected project.

Start here: EATMS System Primer — Free Bundle
https://eatms.gumroad.com/l/dyvzbw

For full catalog or inquiries: eatms.me

Free survival booklet + EATMS updates: email "EATMS" to eatms@pm.me

Please feel free to burn part or all of this book, safely, as an effigy.

www.ingramcontent.com/pod-product-compliance
Lightning Source LLC
LaVergne TN
LVHW050959080826
845145LV00009B/2372

9781966014089